As God Sees

Stepping in From Glory

Noelle Huether

Visit our Website at: AsGodSees.com

Cover and Book Design by Randy Williamson
www.randywilliamson.com

Cover Photo Image by Corina Huether

© Copyright 2016 by Trailblazer Outreach Marketing

The material in this book appears in ebook and book versions of this title:

ebook ISBN 978-0-9977243-1-8

paperback ISBN 978-0-9977243-0-1

i

TERMS OF USE

A word from the publisher about the Bible Translation used.

The World English Bible (WEB) is a Public Domain (no copyright) Modern English translation of the Holy Bible. That means that you may freely copy it in any form, including electronic and print formats. The World English Bible is based on the American Standard Version of the Holy Bible first published in 1901, the Biblia Hebraica Stutgartensa Old Testament, and the Greek Majority Text New Testament. The companion Deuterocanon/ Apocrypha is derived from the Revised Version Apocrypha and the Brenton translation of the Septuagint into English. It is in draft form, and currently being edited for accuracy and readability. The 66 books of the Old and New Testaments are essentially completed, although some proofreading comments are still being accepted when they improve accuracy, readability, and consistency.

WORLD OUTREACH MINISTRIES
PO BOX B
MARIETTA, GA 30061-0379
USA

All emphasis in Scripture has been added by the author.

In the beginning was the Word, and the Word was with God, and the Word was God. The same was in the beginning with God. All things were made through him. Without him was not anything made that has been made. In him was life, and the life was the light of men. The light shines in the darkness, and the darkness hasn't overcome it.

- John 1:1-5 (WEB)

Most certainly I tell you, whoever will not receive God's Kingdom like a little child, he will in no way enter into it.

- Mark 10:15 (WEB)

Dedication

I dedicate this book with warmest affection and prayers to my family, Terry, Corina and Morgen.

You have faithfully and lovingly been patient with me through the years on this project and have encouraged me to go beyond all self-proclaimed limitations upon myself and God. I am grateful beyond words for each one of you.

I also dedicate this book to all the youth who will have the inclination to pick it up. You are the workmanship of a wonderful God who has a specific plan for your life and offers you everything you will ever need to accomplish that plan. Believe in Jesus, trust Him, fight for Him and His truth with all you can muster. As you do, take everyone you possibly can, young and old, with you all the way to Heaven's gates! I pray to meet you there.

Blessings upon you and your journey!

Noelle Huether

ACKNOWLEDGMENTS

I acknowledge Jesus Christ first and foremost because He loved me and chose me before I knew Him. He deserves all my love, praise and honor, for He alone is the source of all that is good in my life. This includes all the people He has strategically placed along my life's journey. My heart swells as I contemplate the numerous individuals who have encouraged, mentored, blessed and breathed grace into me, even at times when I did not deserve it. The pages of this book alone would not be able to contain the names of each individual who has had a profound impact on my life. I struggle with the thought of not putting their names here, but the readers and publisher request only a short list. Thus, I want to thank Lila Clay for your daily encouragement, constant testing, constructive critique and faithfulness through this entire project. You believed in me more than I did. Heartfelt gratitude to my church families of First Church of God, Marion, South Dakota and Northpointe Church of God, Nacogdoches, Texas. Your love, acceptance and mercy have brought me healing, strength, and joy I never thought possible. Thank you Michelle Fink and family for walking for so many years with me on my faith journey regardless of my failures and shortcomings. Thank you Kathy Schmidt for all your encouragement and excitement for this project. Thank you Don and Kim Harper for laying the foundation in me to allow the work of the Holy Spirit in my life in a way that blew past any expectations I could have ever imagined! Thank you my dear brother, Matt Schroer, for your testimony and joy in God speaks to me in ways you will never know. Deepest gratitude to Iva Becker for your long patience with me in this project. Your friendship, wisdom and help in editing is a most generous gift that I humbly receive.

TABLE OF CONTENTS

Introduction

Many say the things of this world are valuable and tremendously important, but I have come to know the fleetingness of all that we see and hold. Thieves rob, death kills, sickness overtakes, and in a moment, our lives can be turned upside down with what seems as no hope in sight. Through the years, I have learned there is one truth that can be clung to which never will be uprooted, destroyed or defeated. That unwavering truth: Jesus Christ is Lord and He alone has the victory!

Regardless of any situation here on earth, which will pass away sooner or later, Jesus walks beside and never leaves those who follow Him in spirit and in truth. This treasure is something that cannot be stolen, cannot be killed (although they did try at one time, but Jesus stepped from the tomb), cannot be destroyed and is worthy of all my effort and time to fight for. This treasure wraps my life in all the promises of Jesus Christ and gives me the surety that I shall live with Him for all eternity.

Regardless of what this world brings to me or what any human can do to me, they can only affect me in this temporal and physical world which will someday pass away.

Even if I had the capacity of great wealth and possessions, nothing would compare to the knowledge and experience of the greatest love and joy that comes from the Creator Himself!

The most powerful testimony of this is from the men and women imprisoned or tortured, now and in times past, while singing from hearts filled with joy to their God who was right there with them.

I marvel at our God who understands firsthand what each one of us is experiencing. All our experiences in the flesh are only for a fleeting moment, but the rewards, the treasures and the joy of this great God last forever! What kind of God is this who still has the victory regardless of what life throws at us? No other god or belief offers the same comfort, hope, joy, love, rewards, personal relationship or eternal salvation than Jesus Christ of Nazareth does who came in the flesh to reconcile all who believe in Him to God the Father, Creator of all that is seen and unseen.

God's Patient Work in My Life

My journey with the Lord began long before I decided to follow Him. As a young girl growing up in a broken home, I struggled in many ways. I remember during a traumatic time at a young age hearing a comforting voice. The voice gently said He loved me as His own child and would always be there for me. I felt as if a gentle and wonderful father was trying to comfort me. I remember saying, "God, is that you?" He answered, "Yes, child, I am here." I was surrounded for a moment with a sense of acceptance, peace, love and joy. As I opened my eyes, I suddenly realized that I was talking to someone I could not see. I quickly dismissed the experience as just wishful thinking coupled with a vivid imagination. Life went back to normal until over a decade later when Jesus revealed Himself again to me in a powerful vision during another painful experience. It was at that moment I decided to follow Jesus because I desperately longed for the peace and love that I experienced with His presence. Thus began my amazing walk with the Lord.

As I grew as a Christian, my relationship with God grew as well as my understanding of His Word, the Bible. There is a long list of wonderful brothers and sisters in Christ who have mentored and discipled me along the way to whom I am greatly indebted. As I sought after God more diligently, He would continue to reveal Himself while reading the Bible, through the encouragement and words of other Christians, through the leading of His Spirit by impressions of peace within, and then, to my surprise, in more direct ways. I began to experience visions, dreams, and God speaking directly to me through my thoughts as well as audibly. This part of the journey was a tough one for me because many Christian leaders and pastors teach that God no longer communicates to His children directly. And yet, these teachings conflict with what Scriptures declare…

"It will happen afterward; that I will pour out my Spirit on all flesh; and your sons and your daughters will prophesy. Your old men will dream dreams. Your young men will see visions." - Joel 2:28, 29 (WEB)

"My sheep hear my voice, and I know them, and they follow me. I give eternal life to them. They will never perish, and no one will snatch them out of my hand." - John 10:27, 28 (WEB)

"But the Counselor, the Holy Spirit, whom the Father will send in my name, he will teach you all things, and will remind you of all that I said to you." - John 14:26 (WEB)

"For who among men knows the things of a man, except the spirit of the man, which is in him?

Even so, no one knows the things of God, except God's Spirit. But we received, not the spirit of the world, but the Spirit which is from God, that we might know the things that were freely given to us by God. Which things also we speak, not in words which man's wisdom teaches, but which the Holy Spirit teaches, comparing spiritual things with spiritual things." - I Corinthians 2:11-13(WEB)

"... Worship God, for the testimony of Jesus is the Spirit of Prophecy." - Revelation 19:10(b)(WEB)

"And when you turn to the right hand, and when you turn to the left, your ears will hear a voice behind you, saying, "This is the way. Walk in it." - Isaiah 30:21 (WEB)

"As for you, the anointing which you received from him remains in you, and you don't need for anyone to teach you. But as his anointing teaches you concerning all things, and is true, and is no lie, and even as it taught you, you will remain in him." - I John 2:27 (WEB)

From Genesis to Revelation, God has revealed Himself to not only His people, but also to nonbelievers such as Darius, Nebuchadnezzar and Saul, who later became Paul. Verses from the Old Testament to the New Testament describe how God speaks to, teaches, guides, encourages and edifies His people. God is the same yesterday, today and tomorrow (see Hebrews 13:8) which means His nature never changes, although His instructions may. There is not one reference in the Bible that says God will withdraw communicating to His people after the Bible is completed. In contrast, Scripture does warn us we can grieve and quench the Spirit as well as deny His work in our lives.

These warnings will be discussed later in this book as well as in the appendix.

Purpose of This Book

My reason for writing this book is foremost an act of obedience to God (Dialogue 1). May these writings encourage, confirm, edify and empower my brothers and sisters in Christ. The dialogues are written as God revealed Himself to me, mainly in parables to which He often explains the meanings.

The messages Jesus shares are not only for me, but for everyone. My prayer is also that many who do not yet know Jesus, will be captivated by His truth and love to choose to have a personal relationship with Him. Salvation is found only in Jesus. For more information on having a personal relationship with Jesus, refer to the appendix.

How to Read the Dialogues

For simplicity and ease of reading, the words 'man' and 'he' are used in the general sense for both male and female. In reading these writings, everything in quotes are the words from either Jesus or God the Father. All other words written are attempts to put into words what I am seeing as well as my thoughts and dialogue with Him. Scripture references relating to the subject of discussion are included in this document. As you engage with each dialogue, start each reading with a prayer of confession (to be right with God), of protection (to keep the enemy's influences away) and of guidance (so the Lord can teach you what He wants you to understand). Then grab your Bible, a writing utensil of choice and begin a study that has the potential to draw you deeper into your relationship with Jesus than you thought possible.

Jesus is the only personal God who desires for all men to come to Him through the offer of friendship.

Salvation is not because of anything great or wonderful or perfect that we have done. On the contrary, salvation is only because of Jesus' perfect life which He offered freely as a sacrifice on the cross. His life, death and resurrection demonstrate to all His great love for us. None of us are worthy on our own accord. We are worthy only because God created each one of us and calls to us to come to Him. (Psalm 139:13-18, Proverbs 1:20-33, I Timothy 2:3-6, John 14:6). The truths God shares in these dialogues are not just for me, they are for everyone who chooses to follow Him.

Dialogue 1

The Glory of Jesus in His Kingdom

"I saw no temple in it, for the Lord God, the Almighty, and the Lamb, are its temple. The city has no need for the sun, neither of the moon, to shine, for the very glory of God illuminated it, and its lamp is the Lamb. The nations will walk in its light. The kings of the earth bring the glory and honor of the nations into it. Its gates will in no way be shut by day (for there will be no night there), and they shall bring the glory and the honor of the nations into it so that they may enter. There will in no way enter into it anything profane, or one who causes an abomination or a lie, but only those who are written in the Lamb's book of life." - Revelation 21:22-27 (WEB)

The Anticipation

"There will in no way enter into it anything profane, or one who causes an abomination or a lie, but only those who are written in the Lamb's book of life." - Revelation 21:27, (WEB)

Why are you reading this book?

Who is Jesus to you? In what areas do you have questions about God?

What is your ultimate goal in life? Read I Thessalonians 4:3-8. Are you willing to reevaluate your life in the light of God's truth and what He desires for you? Why or why not?

The Conversation

"Come." I see an expression of playfulness and joy upon His face. "You, My child, have sought Me earnestly. Seek Me more diligently. Hang onto what I have already given you. Do not displace what I have placed in your hands, in your mouth, and in your heart. Remember, cling to what is truth, meditate upon these things. My Word endures to the end."

I see what looks like transparent layers of words and images stacked on top of each other. They are slightly offset from one another. The words and the images seem to be in contradiction, yet they are in perfect harmony. As I study the vision I hear the Lord speak.

"My Words will stand, in perfect harmony and in perfect understanding. You see, in man's perspective, all is linear, maybe even circular as some would define, but in truth, My words are endless, spoken from eternity into time."

I realize I am suddenly standing outside of what I know as time. I watch as what looks like light from eternity shines into the world's timeline at three different points. What comes from the same source from eternity is delivered within man's time differently, like each one building upon the one before.

"Truly, men from within time cannot comprehend My existence outside their realm. All they comprehend will go through their filter which is interdependent on time. Only through My Holy Spirit and My direction, may they receive a glimpse of who I am, and of My truth. They must be willing to let Me reveal Myself as I am and not who they want Me to be. Although many seek more understanding, often it is for their gain, their private interpretation to build and defend their ideas. Thus, in their pride and arrogance, they take shadows of My truth to design their own god. Then as they teach their human understanding as truth, they destroy the lives of others. No, only the pure in heart shall see My glory, My truth and My Kingdom. Purity is only wrought in humility covered with My atoning sacrifice. Know this, those who have tasted of My glory or My truth as I revealed Myself to them shall not be welcome in My kingdom when they walk away after their own ambitions and worldly desires that are not of Me. They shall be judged according to their own judgments upon others in the light of My law. My law is as I lived, it is denying self and loving with a pure heart. And this," He gestures towards the city, "Is My city."

We walk towards the gates which are emitting tremendous brilliance and light. No human eye can gaze upon their brightness for blindness would be the result. The light permeates my being, flowing through me and filling me. Anything that is in me that is not of God is burned away to where I shine as bright as the city.

As we enter into the gates, Jesus seems to shine even brighter and grow in majesty, if that was even possible. The city does not have walls or boundaries as we understand on earth. Still, I recognize that is how my mind is interpreting what I see for there is no other way to comprehend the scenes before me. Jesus just is. He is all in all. His glory is penetrating every speck of this realm. Again I am struck by the ramifications of rejection. Anyone who rejects Jesus on earth cannot come here. Not only would his sin not be allowed to remain here, he would not be able to stand anywhere in God's Kingdom. Rejection of Jesus in our realm is rejection of Him in all realms. How can anyone who does not know Him as Lord stand before Him here, within the gates of His own city?

The city goes on in every direction as far as I can see. I am starting to distinguish colors now. The colors are not as we see here on earth, but shine as if the colors are light with substance and intensity.

"My realm in its fullness is the essence of My existence. All that is truth, My truth, exists beyond the effects of man or evil. The evil one can only influence the perception of man in order to kill, steal and destroy that which I created. I desire to bring all that I have made unto Myself, yet I give man free will. The choice is for man to love Me in return. This city, all of My realms beyond the sphere of creation, is the fullness of My promises. Here, there is no more pain, sin, jealousies, angst, fear, or any form of evil or death."

Jesus turns to look at me. "Share what you have seen. Write what you have heard. Stand regardless of what the world says. You cannot be removed from Me, but you can choose to deny Me and walk away from all I have for you."

I kneel before the King of Kings. I choose You, Lord. Thank You for choosing me.

Dialogue 2

The Shepherd of Life Speaks

"Most certainly, I tell you, one who doesn't enter by the door into the sheep fold, but climbs up some other way, the same is a thief and a robber. But one who enters in by the door is the shepherd of the sheep. The gatekeeper opens the gate for him, and the sheep listen to his voice. He calls his own sheep by name, and leads them out. Whenever he brings out his own sheep, he goes before them, and the sheep follow him, for they know his voice. They will by no means follow a stranger, but will flee from him; for they don't know the voice of strangers." Jesus spoke this parable to them, but they didn't understand what he was telling them.

Jesus therefore said to them again, "Most certainly, I tell you, I am the sheep's door. All who came before me are thieves and robbers, but the sheep didn't listen to them. I am the door. If anyone enters in by me, he will be saved, and will go in and go out, and will find pasture." - John 10:1-9, (WEB)

The Anticipation

"My sheep hear my voice, and I know them, and they follow me." - John 10:27 (WEB)

What is keeping you from hearing God's voice?

In what areas of your life are you struggling with doubt?

The Conversation

The world around me begins to fade as the light of His truth and Word begins to take root and grow in my heart and mind. I feel His peace wrap around me as I sense the King of glory's presence. Who can deny His power and majesty? I humble myself in His presence. As He draws closer, He reveals Himself in my mind like a vision or a dream. He sits down beside me, as a vast meadow is displayed before us. As far as my eyes can see are rolling hills covered in lush, green grass with delicate flowers waving gently in the breeze. I look closer at the vibrancy of the flowers' colors, amazed at their intensity and clarity. I marvel at the beauty of purity and life around me and how it fills me with a sense of provision as well as safety. I turn to Jesus. How can I even describe Him? His presence is a complex web of human paradoxes, and yet, as I gaze upon Him, I realize He is complete perfection in order and reason. He directs my attention to the meadow before us. His splendor and glory radiates so intensely that not one shadow dares to make its presence.

In the meadow, I see a large group of people begin to appear as if superimposed or transparent on the grass. The large gathering of people seems to shift so as to display different cultures from around the world, each one separated within faded circles. I sense that all the circles are somehow interlinked with one another.

"Child, I love you. I love them too. They do not hear My voice as sheep would hear their shepherd's. They cannot hear Me over the roar of the world, over the lies of the enemy or even over the hurt of others. Do you see them?"

As I look more intently upon the people, I see a few individuals shining brightly among the crowds. They are trying to speak to the others as if they have something very important to say. I look to Jesus for understanding.

"The people with My light within them are trying to tell the others, to warn them. Look closer."

As I turn my gaze back to the people, I notice bits of black or specks of darkness in many of the people who have Jesus' light shining in them.

"They are unable to hear Me. They hear the roar of the world, the pain of others, and the lies of the enemy. At the same time they also feel My presence and know I am truth. Many of them allow their feelings to become very intense as they walk among the people. They are walking in confusion and chaos."

I turn to question Jesus, could You not just find a way to talk to them?

"I have tried to speak to them. They only desire what truth I can give them that fits into their understanding of Me and My word."

"You may think I cannot use you for many reasons you could list, including your past, but I have created you. I have protected you and brought you through. Your faith and desire for Me and My truth, regardless of what it may be, has brought you here. Now you are next to Me, on this hill, looking at My People. Because you have been made clean through My blood and your obedience is to My Father, I can use you for His glory. Stay pure, stay holy, stay right here, next to Me and with Father. When I send you, do as I lead you and then run back to Me."

He then sends me to the people below. I see myself walking into the different circles nestled in the meadow. Jesus is with me, giving me the words to speak and the love to give. I can feel His love flow through me to love all those I meet. I feel protected and empowered as long as I keep my eyes on Him. When I finish His will, I come back to sit with Him alone, once again, on the hillside. Before I can sit though, He brushes me off and cleanses me. I realize all Jesus is asking me to do is to love Him, love others, and to obey and trust Him. He does everything else!

Then I see myself run to the Father as a child. (Ephesians 2:18, Hebrews 4:14-16) He is happy to receive me. There truly is only one way to the Father, through Jesus Christ our Lord! (John 14:6)

Dialogue 3

The False Shepherd Brings Death

"The thief only comes to steal, kill, and destroy. I came that they may have life, and may have it abundantly. I am the good shepherd. The good shepherd lays down his life for the sheep. He who is a hired hand, and not a shepherd, who doesn't own the sheep, sees the wolf coming, leaves the sheep, and flees. The wolf snatches the sheep, and scatters them. The hired hand flees because he is a hired hand, and doesn't care for the sheep. I am the good shepherd. I know my own, and I'm known by my own; even as the Father knows me, and I know the Father. I lay down my life for the sheep. I have other sheep, which are not of this fold. I must bring them also, and they will hear my voice. They will become one flock with one shepherd." - John 10:10-16 (WEB)

The Anticipation

"I have other sheep, which are not of this fold. I must bring them also, and they will hear my voice. They will become one flock with one shepherd." - John 10:16 (WEB)

We all have a need to know the truth. How would you recognize truth? What is truth to you?

If God revealed something to you would you be ready to listen? Do you desire truth in your life?

The Conversation

"Do you see the sheep?"

Yes, they are healthy and white. Calm, eating lush pasture.

"See the shepherd with them?"

Yes, lanky and dark. He is very thin and tall.

"He is not mine. The sheep are Mine. They trust him as if he was Me."

What is his intent?

"He is seducing them. He is fattening them up for the slaughter house." For a moment, I see a white wooden building with a single door on the right side. I smell a profuse odor as the door opens and see the white washed walls leading to what I understand as death below.

"They do not even look, really look at him. If they did they would see his eyes, his desire to do them evil. His darkness flows around him. The sheep only feed themselves and see the grass in front of them. He makes sure they are always in a pasture of desirable food."

Lord, can they receive Your truth even with a bad shepherd?

"Only if they desire truth. Many no longer see the value of My love, My truth or My gifts. They perceive Me as desiring to do them harm, to make them starve. This is their perception of Me." I see Jesus standing, for a brief moment, on drought land. His glory and beauty emphasize even more the barrenness of the dusty dry ground around Him.

In contrast, the rich meadow surrounding His sheep is filled with many good things. As the peace of the meadow flows through me, I proclaim, Lord, Your provision, Your love, and Your desire for us is so much more!

Jesus points to the sheep, "See that one?" I see a young sheep, about half grown. He is looking around, completely aware of all that is happening. He takes a bite, looks at the others, walks around a bit. He looks at the lanky shepherd with trepidation. He eats and acts like he is one of the rest when the shepherd's eyes are on him.

"The young sheep is looking for the truth, but does not know where to go to find it. He has no idea what he is looking for. He does not even see Me. The others have not told him about Me. He is the one to whom I am calling. He can hear My voice faintly, so much so he doubts if he hears Me at all."

What must be done, Lord?

"Each one has a seed within. A seed, a desire, not a hole, but a longing within that only I can fulfill to a fullness beyond his understanding. The older sheep are trying to satisfy that with the pleasures and rewards of this world. Others avoid Me for either fear of the false shepherd or fear of their perception of who I am. Keep loving and teaching the young one who in turn will feed the others. Then I will be made complete in him."

A moment later, I watch in horror as the false shepherd attacks the young one.

"Truth, the young one needs truth. Truth to fight for Me. Truth to fight for himself. Truth to fight for others. When he can stand empowered by My Love and Spirit, he will love Me, himself and others. Then the enemy and the world will have no power over him."

I shiver at the earnestness in Jesus' voice.

Dialogue 4

Ties That Bind

"I am the true vine, and my Father is the farmer. Every branch in me that doesn't bear fruit, he takes away. Every branch that bears fruit, he prunes, that it may bear more fruit. You are already pruned clean because of the word which I have spoken to you. Remain in me, and I in you. As the branch can't bear fruit by itself, unless it remains in the vine, so neither can you, unless you remain in me. I am the vine. You are the branches. He who remains in me, and I in him, the same bears much fruit, for apart from me you can do nothing. If a man doesn't remain in me, he is thrown out as a branch, and is withered; and they gather them, throw them into the fire, and they are burned. If you remain in me, and my words remain in you, you will ask whatever you desire, and it will be done for you.

"In this is my Father glorified, that you bear much fruit; and so you will be my disciples. Even as the Father has loved me, I also have loved you. Remain in my love." - John 15:1-9 (WEB)

The Anticipation

"I am the vine. You are the branches. He who remains in me, and I in him, the same bears much fruit, for apart from me you can do nothing." - John 15:5 (WEB)

Have you ever thought much about how we are connected to God and each other? How have your choices impacted the lives of others for better or worse?

What do you need to do to make better choices? Are there things that you need to turn away from in order to make better choices not only for yourself but for others? Think about this.

The Conversation

As we continue to look upon the sheep on the meadow, "You are missing something."

What am I missing, Lord? Reveal it to me.

The scene before us darkens ever so slightly as thin connections between the sheep begin to appear. The lines or threads also connect the sheep to the bad shepherd. The connections between God and those who chose Him are thicker and brighter in comparison to the rest. Those connected to God are brightly connected to each other as well as the young ones.

"Understand this, that which is from Me returns to Me. That which is not of Me, will not follow Me. They cannot go where I am. Remember where it says, 'One must leave mother, brother, father, children for My name's sake.' Also, 'Let the dead bury the dead.'"

"Everyone who has left houses, or brothers, or sisters, or father, or mother, or wife, or children, or lands, for my name's sake, will receive one hundred times, and will inherit eternal life." - Matthew 19:29 (WEB)

"But Jesus said to him, 'Follow me, and leave the dead to bury their own dead.'" - Matthew 8:22 (WEB)

Jesus continues, "Forsake the world and all that is in it. The world's ties are attached to people until the ties are forsaken for My name's sake. Those ties cause chaos within the lives of many. They must learn to understand how the things of this world impact them: the lust of the eyes, the lust of the flesh and the pride of life. My sheep are not only hurting themselves, but those to whom they are connected." (See I John 2:16)

As He was speaking I began to recall His words in the Gospel of John.

"He who loves his life will lose it. He who hates his life in this world will keep it to eternal life. If anyone serves me, let him follow me. Where I am, there will my servant also be. If anyone serves me, the Father will honor him" - John 12:25, 26 (WEB)

"They need to know that each one chooses the tie that binds. Mine is of love. The enemy's is of fear."

Dialogue 5

True Rest

All things have been delivered to me by my Father. No one knows the Son, except the Father; neither does anyone know the Father, except the Son, and he to whom the Son desires to reveal him. "Come to me, all you who labor and are heavily burdened, and I will give you rest. Take my yoke upon you, and learn from me, for I am gentle and humble in heart; and you will find rest for your souls. For my yoke is easy, and my burden is light." - Matthew 11:27-30 (WEB)

The Anticipation

"Come to me, all you who labor and are heavily burdened, and I will give you rest." - Matthew 11:28 (WEB)

When was the last time you rested? Did you feel guilty about taking the time to do nothing? Describe where you were and how you felt.

What do you think it means to rest in Jesus? Have you ever considered the fact that Jesus longs to be your friend as well as your God and Savior?

The Conversation

"Come here, child." He stands up, takes my hand and I follow His leading. As we walk along a pristine beach I notice the tall rock cliffs wrap around the beach on all sides. A sense of safety and peace flow over me like the light breeze in the air. I feel the warmth of the white sand beneath my feet. The gentle sound of waves rolling on the shoreline drifts to my ears. I am amazed at the clarity of the clear blue water before us. The sun is warm and shines brightly in a clear sky. "Child, do you know why I brought you here?"

No, Lord.

"This is a safe place. Away from the world you know, secluded, safe, warm, and beautiful. Close your eyes. Feel the warmth. Smell the air. Can you?"

Yes, Lord, I can!

"When all that is around you is peace, rest in it. Don't just run off and busy yourself. Rest. Receive, enjoy, and accept the goodness I desire to bestow upon you. Dwell in My gift. Dwell with Me."

How long? How much?

"As long as I allow you to. I will tell you when it is time to move on. I may have for you a lesson or a discussion. Enjoy with every sense. Let Me fill your body, soul, and mind with My peace and joy as you rest."

I rest next to my Lord on the beach away from all the cares, burdens, and pain of the world. I realize I am in His presence so I began to think of anything I may have done wrong so that I can confess it.

He looks at me, smiles, put His finger to His mouth for silence and says, "Not now child. Just be with me. You are Mine." I accept His guidance and begin to enjoy just being beside Him.

"You see, I desire to be more than your Lord, more than your God, and more than your Savior. I also desire to be your friend; one you love, trust and desire to be with. So many come to me with burdens, prayers, confessions and yes, I am the One who loves them as their Lord and Savior. Yet, I desire to be so much more. I desire to walk side by side with them as their friend, the closest friend they could ever want. Complete and total unconditional love I have to give to each who desires to receive Me."

His words from John 15:15 come to mind where Jesus calls us friends. I desire, Lord, for You to be totally and completely mine and for me to be totally and completely Yours as You have designed. Teach me how to be Yours.

Jesus smiles. "Friendship is both ways, is it not? What you desire in our relationship is very important too. I will not push Myself upon you in a way you do not want or are uncomfortable with. It's like a dance. One of respect, love, trust, communication, time, and one of patience."

I continue to rest beside my Friend, thanking Him for His greatness and wonderful love.

Dialogue 6

Understanding God's Way

"He said to them, "This is what I told you, while I was still with you, that all things which are written in the law of Moses, the prophets, and the psalms, concerning me must be fulfilled. Then he opened their minds, that they might understand the Scriptures."" - *Luke 24:44, 45 (WEB)*

The Anticipation

"Then he opened their minds, that they might understand the Scriptures." - *Luke 24: 45 (WEB)*

What is your greatest desire in life?

Did you include understanding the Bible better in your answer? When you read the Scriptures do you understand what you are reading? In what areas of the Bible do you struggle to understand?

What can you do to understand God's word better?

The Conversation

Glorious Father, King of all Kings, Lord of all my being, for You created all that is seen and unseen. You created all from beginning to the end. You alone have all authority in Heaven and on earth. Father, send Your Spirit to teach and to guide. Protect me and my thoughts from the enemy as well as my own understanding. Jesus, my Lord, my Savior, my truest Friend, be my truth and protection. Your servant is listening.

"What is your desire?"

Your will for me. I desire to walk in Your way, to do as You would will for my life, to be faithful and true to Your purpose for this life You have given me. I desire to stay on the path You have lit with Your Word and Spirit.

"Child, it is not like you are to guess and search out that one correct answer from Me for your life. I know the end from the beginning. I know My plan for you. I shall accomplish My work in you. You only need to love and obey Me. All that is not done in faith is sin. If you go the wrong way, be assured I will bring you back to the path I have for you. It is not a matter of what you do for Me, but what I do through you. Desire to please Me." (See Romans 14:23b, John 8:29)

I start to feel doubt. Is this a true desire of my heart now? And even if it is, how would I ever be able to please Him? Jesus wraps Himself around me and fills me with His glory. The doubt fades as vapor below my feet.

"Desire to please Me, which you know can only be done My way, not through the way of the world. You prayed this morning for Me to open your understanding to My Word. It shall be fulfilled in you."

Lord, my heart sings with joy and anticipation at the thought! How can I thank you enough for such a gift? Let my understanding be Your understanding, my thoughts be Your thoughts, my ways Your ways so that all I speak and do is Your truth revealed. Give me wisdom in teaching, so others may understand.

I begin to pray for anyone who would hear me, that they would understand, but Jesus corrects me. "My truth is only for those who desire to know Me. Just as My parables were hidden from the masses, so will My truth be now. I hide My truth from those who do not want Me." Then He shows me how all of eternity will be filled with Him. I understand immediately that a person who does not want to be near Jesus during his or her lifetime could not stand to be in eternity with Him where not one speck of heaven will be shadowed from His glory.

"None can see My face and live. That is why one must die to themselves to live. One must surrender their lives for the life I will give them. One must choose whom he or she will serve." (See Matthew 16:25)

Dialogue 7

Loving Completely

"Jesus answered, "The greatest is, 'Hear, Israel, the Lord our God, the Lord is one: you shall love the Lord your God with all your heart, and with all your soul, and with all your mind, and with all your strength.' This is the first commandment." - Mark 12:29, 30 (WEB)

The Anticipation

"You shall love the Lord your God with all your heart, and with all your soul, and with all your mind, and with all your strength.' This is the first commandment. - Mark 12:30 (WEB)

Do you love Him? Do you love the Lord with all your heart, soul, mind and strength? What does that look like? What are the obstacles in your life that keep you from loving Him?

Read Luke 14:25-30. Hate is a strong word, what do you think He means? Does he really want us to hate, when we have been told to love others?

Now read Mark 10:29, 30. This Scripture says that we will receive 100 times as much as we give up when we follow Jesus. Why do you think we are so richly rewarded? (See Matthew 6:33 for the answer.)

The Conversation

Jesus, I desire to speak only Your truth. To know Your truth so fully that there would be no lies or darkness or fear or deceit in me.

"Is that truly what you desire?" He asks.

Suddenly I had the impression that I can have His wisdom and understanding fill all of me, but if I do there would be none of the world's wisdom or understanding. I realize I would be ignorant of the ways of the world and its workings. I contemplated the separation from the understandings of the world versus those of God. Ideally, I desire full understanding of both, Lord.

"It cannot work that way, child. It is one or the other, you can only have both to a certain level of understanding but not to their fullness. What you are requesting, child, is My glory, My truth to fill all of you. There can be nothing else in you. You truly will be separated from the world. You will be set apart, sanctified entirely unto Me and My purpose."

May I ask what Your desire for me would be? What would please You?

"Love Me with all your heart. Love Me with all your soul. Love Me with all your mind. Love Me with all your strength."

Lord, if you desire all, I ...

"You must mean what you say. Let your 'yes' be 'yes'."

As I gaze into the eyes of the Lord and Savior of all generations, the One who lived and died for me, the One whose love for me surpasses all understanding I could ever have, My Jesus, My Lord...

"Do you love Me more than them?" My mind begins to wander to my family and friends. Yes, my Lord, my God, I love you more. Only You have the words of life. Only You can save me from this flesh. Only You can free me from all bondage and slavery of this world. You, alone, not only hold eternity in Your hand, but also fill it with Your Glory at the same time. Yes, Jesus Christ, I desire to have You and You alone fill all of me. Let there be nothing else left in me, nothing of the world, nothing not of You. Remove every memory or thought or feeling or belief that cannot stand in the light of Your glory. I only want You. If I am ostracized, hated or rejected for Your Name's sake, may I rejoice! May the fear and trembling I have before men, be submitted to You and You alone. May it be changed to an earnest desire to do Your perfect will and become an expectation of abiding in You every minute of every day. May You change my fears to an overflowing of Your Spirit to please and love You with my whole heart, soul, mind and strength. Keep reminding me, keep me obedient, keep me submissive to You, keep me empowered for and by You. I desire You and Your Glory to fill me completely, pressed down, shaken and overflowing, filled with Your life. I am Yours, Jesus Christ of Nazareth.

Dialogue 8

His Light Shines in Us

"But the path of the righteous is like the dawning light, that shines more and more until the perfect day. The way of the wicked is like darkness. They don't know what they stumble over. My son, attend to my words. Turn your ear to my sayings. Let them not depart from your eyes. Keep them in the center of your heart. For they are life to those who find them, and health to their whole body. Keep your heart with all diligence, for out of it is the wellspring of life. Put away from yourself a perverse mouth. Put corrupt lips far from you. Let your eyes look straight ahead. Fix your gaze directly before you. Make the path of your feet level. Let all of your ways be established. Don't turn to the right hand nor to the left. Remove your foot from evil." - Proverbs 4:18-27 (WEB)

The Anticipation

But the path of the righteous is like the dawning light, that shines more and more until the perfect day. - Proverbs 4:18 (WEB)

Have you considered how your life is so important and valued that God desires to shine His light through you? How would your life look different if God's light shined more in your life?

Standing where you are at in your life right now, where would you like more of God's light in your life?

In Proverbs 4 above, we are told we must remove ourselves from evil. What areas or things in your life would be dishonoring or considered evil in God's eyes that need to be removed? Are you willing to surrender these things to Jesus and ask for His help to have the victory in these areas?

The Conversation

"Cast the stone in your hand."

I realize there is a small stone in my hand; it is smooth, round, and oblong.

A brilliant light shines upon the stone to reveal that it is white with small specklings on it. I notice the light that is shining upon it is refracting to radiate upon my whole hand. I ask Jesus if I am seeing correctly.

He nods.

Shall I toss it now?

"Yes, child."

I raise my hand wondering what to expect. I toss it before me into the darkness. It flies through the air in slow motion. As it soars through the air, it lights the space around it. I see glimpses of the surroundings, but not enough to distinguish anything clearly. I watch as the stone lands softly in the distance and begins to fade. I sense a coldness to the stone as its light dies away.

"Here, try this one." The Lord hands me another stone. It is similar to the first one, but slightly larger.

"Drop this one before you."

It also has light emanating from within it. I hold it out before me and let it drop to the ground. It falls to the ground and bounces to the right. As it does, once again I can see the small area around it lit up, but still unable to distinguish or recognize anything specific. Just as the first stone, it too becomes dark and cold.

"Here take these." He places many small rocks in my cupped hands. They are all lit up as well, but together their light is stronger. I hold them up before me to let their lights shine. The immediate area all around me lights up just like it does when Jesus is near. As I look back at the lights in my hands, I become aware that they somehow represent lives radiating God's glory. I earnestly look up at Jesus, Oh Lord, I do not want to hurt them.

"Child, feel them."

I close my eyes and let their light radiate around me. I feel heat and power on my hands, similar to the glory that flows from Jesus. I also can sense a love for them and from them. I understand the unity in Jesus we have with each other and Him. Then suddenly I am aware of something drastically different. I can feel their busyness and anxiety of life.

Lord, they are so busy. Do they not know? I ask as I hand them to Him. They seem heavier than when He first placed them within my hands.

"I desire to love My people. I desire to share with them all the wonderful gifts I have for them. But just as you tossed and dropped the stones I gave you, they do the same to Me. They take Me and My truth, hold it for a bit, then toss it away or drop it. Then they walk away leaving all I had given them." (See I Samuel 3:19-21)

"This is what I want to do for them," I can feel His love with just a glance from His eyes. Even though His love is extremely intense and powerful, it is also gentle. He touches me. I sense His light traveling from my shoulder and flowing through me to every part of my being till I shine all around and see clearly everything around me. The colors are beyond description! The brilliance is almost blinding! The joy within is so intense I feel I could explode! I can see people in the distance laughing and fellowshipping together in unity and freedom. As I watch them, the darkness flees from before me. A moment later I sense the darkness try to fight its way back around me, but I put my trust in my Lord to do what He started in me. His peace continues to flow through me.

I turn around and see different rooms with transparent walls. Inside each area I see a wide variety of activities, people, events and life experiences. Each area is different, yet all are lit up clearly. I feel no fear or doubt, just love for God and for the people all around us.

"This is My truth. You can see clearly, you can understand fully, and you can walk without stumbling when My light and truth is allowed to manifest within you."

Yes, Lord, there is no darkness now, I can see clearly. I know I cannot do this on my own, help me to stay near You. May You bring this unity to all

Your people. May we all know Your love for one another so You will be glorified.

Dialogue 9

God's Love is Essential for Unity

"Not for these only do I pray, but for those also who believe in me through their word, that they may all be one; even as you, Father, are in me, and I in you, that they also may be one in us; that the world may believe that you sent me. The glory which you have given me, I have given to them; that they may be one, even as we are one; I in them, and you in me, that they may be perfected into one; that the world may know that you sent me, and loved them, even as you loved me." - John 17:20-23 (WEB)

The Anticipation

"The glory which you have given me, I have given to them; that they may be one, even as we are one" - John 17: 22 (WEB)

If you were in the upper room that day and heard Jesus pray for you, how would you feel? Would you feel more confident, bolder, better? Now what if I told you that Jesus was praying for you in that upper room. Do time and distance really make that much of a difference? Why or why not?

Insert your name in the following prayer Jesus prayed in John 17:20-26 as you do consider the implications of this prayer and the authority of the one who prayed it.

"Not for these only do I pray, but for (insert) also who believes in me through their word, that (insert) may also be one; even as you, Father, are in me, and I in you, that (insert) also may be one in us; that the world may believe that you sent me. The glory which you have given me, I have given to (insert); that (insert) may be one, even as we are one; I in (insert), and you in me, that (insert) may be perfected into one; that the world may know that you sent me, and loved (insert), even as you loved me. Father, I desire that (insert) also whom you have given me be with me where I am, that (insert) may see my glory, which you have given me, for you loved me before the foundation of the world. Righteous Father, the world hasn't known you, but I knew you; and (insert) knew that you sent me. I made known to (insert) your name, and will make it known; that the love with which you loved me may be in (insert), and I in (insert)."

The Conversation

The Lord hands me a green jewel. What is this Lord? As I examine the jewel, I have a sense that green means abundant life.

"Hold it, look at it. Feel it. Feel it with your spirit for it is from Me."

I am holding it. It is bright with rays of green shining from its center to the space around it making my hands a beautiful translucent emerald green. I peer into the jewel letting it transform itself in my hands. I see my two children. Both of them are glowing brightly with laughter and love flowing from them. Their light shines around them on my hands.

Lord, these two are beautiful treasures from You. They are wonderful gifts from You. You have blessed them as well as me. They have been patient with me and forgiven me so much. I treasure them as a gift from You, yet I know, they are Yours first and Yours last. You are their God, Savior, and Lord. They truly belong to You. You love them more than I. You created their very beings and souls for Your pleasure and perfect will. Lord, how can I love them and treasure them as a gift of love from You, and still place them in Your hands? They are Yours. I want You to protect them, I cannot protect them well enough. I want You to provide for them, love them, cherish them, guide them, teach them, for You are greater than I.

"You are My child. I live in you, and so does My Word. Abide in Me and I will abide in you. Now, stop. Experience Me in you and you in Me. According to the world, this is impossible on many levels. First, I am God, you are human. Secondly, how can one who is in something have that which he is in be in them? Oh, how fickle man is. The world that people have created in their own minds is also the world they are in - the world they perceive and journey in. You have heard it said that one's perception is one's truth. So it is here. When I and My Word abide in you, then My Word is your perception, your truth. Remember, My truth is the standard. To walk in any other way is false. It is a lie, deceit and darkness for there is no darkness in Me, only light which is the truth."

"Now, if others - let's start with children from you and your husband - also abide in Me and I abide in them, what manner of relationship do you have with them? Are they not now abiding with you and you with them as you all abide in Me? Child, all that is within Me has the assurance of My promises and My love. John 17 gives you a glimpse of this unity that humans can have with Me, My Father, and with each other. I was given My disciples as a gift from My Father. I, in return, submitted Myself to Him and to them. By doing this, each one was still My Father's glory, and yet, Mine to love, cherish, teach and empower. I was also, because of the truth of My love, able to present them to My Father as a gift of love to them and to Him. You see, all is My Father's, all is in His control. And yet, with what measure of love you receive from Us and pour into other's lives, these are the treasures you will present before Me and your Father as a token of your love for Us."

"Our love is more powerful than man can imagine. Not only is it powerful in your life, it is tremendously powerful when poured into the lives around you. We desire for man to receive Our love to the perfect measure as We have designed each to receive. You see, man was not only created to love Us, but he was created to be loved by Us. The presence of Our Spirit within his life brings an ever-increasing amount of Our glory to penetrate the body, soul and mind of the believer. As our love and truth increases within him, which also means to say the Spirit and Our glory, any darkness within him is carefully cleansed away."

Dialogue 10

Love Without Fear

"Because we are members of his body, of his flesh and bones. 'For this cause a man will leave his father and mother, and will be joined to his wife. The two will become one flesh.' This mystery is great, but I speak concerning Christ and of the assembly." - Ephesians 5:30-32 (WEB)

The Anticipation

"This mystery is great, but I speak concerning Christ and of the assembly." - Ephesians 5:32 (WEB)

Imagine the greatest love found on earth. What did you picture? The love of a mother for her child, and dad for his kid, or did you see a young couple exchanging vows? How are these expressions of love different from each other? How do you think they differ from God's love?

If you are married, do you and your spouse seek God together? Why or why not?

If you could experience God at a more intimate level, would you want to? What obstacles would you face for a greater level of understanding? What if God desired to draw closer to you? Would you let Him come near?

The Conversation

Father, speak Your truth about the love You desire Your children to know and share here on earth in Your name. I have hugged friends dear to me who love You and feel an intimacy, a love that is unknown to me. I have also been near other Christians or shook their hands and felt a power, a flow of energy that is beyond anything this world can explain. Is this of You?

"My child. Quiet your heart, your mind, your spirit. Be still and just know

Me and My love. Just be for a moment, just with Me."

As I silence myself and rest with Him, He draws near. I am surrounded with light, power, joy and love indescribable. My whole being is filled to where I can barely draw a breath. My body trembles as His presence is more than I can contain. Oh, to walk in this love; moment by moment. To touch another with just a drop of His glory within would surely be enough to heal body, soul and mind. At this moment my faith is at a level where I know anything is possible with God. He truly does summon that which does not exist as if it does. (See Romans 4:16, 17)

What I am experiencing is like a Niagara Water Fall of the river of love compared to what I experience with my closest Christian friends. I have never experienced any semblance of this even within a physical context with my Christian husband. I am acknowledging this love, this intimacy is different from the human understanding of love in all areas: physically and emotionally.

In I Peter 4:8 (WEB) the Apostle Paul reminds us *"And above all things be earnest in your love among yourselves, for love covers a multitude of sins."*

Father, in the case of a husband and wife where the husband loves his wife so much, if love has the power to heal, why would a man's love for his wife not be enough to heal her? Then I ask the Lord to show me what a person's love for another is normally like in contrast to the pure, holy love from the glory of God's spirit. I immediately see iron bars, like a prison, thick and black. Words like desperate, fear, hopelessness, flash before me. Then I sense a feeling of grasping at thin air or straws.

"The love humans know and experience many times is one mingled with fear. This fear may be based on one's understanding of pain, self protection or desires. It may also stem from roots in one's life from their past or failings. There is also another element of love mingled with fear: the unknown. Man's understanding is limited in ways beyond his comprehension. People see with their eyes a way that seems right to them and then respond. The way of fear is not the way of faith. One may love deeply, but there is almost always an element of fear mingled in, this causes bondage to a degree beyond expectation. My love contains no fear, for I not only know all things, but am holy, pure and above all things. The closer one walks with Me, the more My love can not only fill him, but also flow through him. The result? A life of pure love, a life of power and clarity, a life walking in holiness which will experience My miracles and wondrous works."

Dialogue 11

Doubt Flies In

Peter answered him and said, "Lord, if it is you, command me to come to you on the waters."

He said, "Come!"

Peter stepped down from the boat, and walked on the waters to come to Jesus. But when he saw that the wind was strong, he was afraid, and beginning to sink, he cried out, saying, "Lord, save me!"

Immediately Jesus stretched out his hand, took hold of him, and said to him, "You of little faith, why did you doubt?" When they got up into the boat, the wind ceased. Those who were in the boat came and worshiped him, saying, "You are truly the Son of God!" - *Matthew 14:28-33 (WEB)*

The Anticipation

"…You of little faith, why did you doubt?" - *Matthew 14:31(b) (WEB)*

Doubt is our enemy. Doubt is like a little bit of infection that can spread through the whole body if left unchecked. It attacks our faith and creates confusion and fear. How has doubt caused you to struggle? Examine the consequences of doubt, review James 1:6-8.

Faith is our answer to doubt. But what is it? Hebrews 11:1 has the answer you can write below.

When you read the words "*I will in no way leave you, neither will I in any way forsake you,*" (Hebrews 13:5b, WEB) do you believe that even when you cannot feel or see God? Why or why not? Pray about it.

The Conversation

Lord Jesus, I praise You for You are holy and true, greater than any understanding I may have of You. And yet, You desire to love us and be loved by us. How can I declare Your goodness? I wait upon You...

"Fight for Me, remember what I have taught you. Focus, strive, seek, for I shall be found by you. Come, child, sit with Me." Jesus leads me to a quiet place near Him. It is bright light all around. Only the Lord is near radiating His glory as we sit on what looks like a blue and white blanket. I feel His glory penetrate into me and shine through my being. As it does, I see my own spirit glow in radiance. I feel like I can float away, but I am held before Him somehow. Lord, I love You. Oh, to be able to love You as You deserve to be loved every minute of every day of my life. I know I don't. Increase my faith, Lord. I desire more of You.

"Just be, be with Me. Not do, not fret, not anything. Just be." As I relax and rest with His presence surrounding me, I am filled with His love and His light. I wait with Him praying that all darkness and sin within me will be cleansed away.

After some time of abiding with Jesus, He says, "Let's talk about doubt, child. You see, doubt is powerful. Even a drop of doubt in the mind will become a flood of doubt in the heart. It is more powerful than any other temptation. It is what Adam and Eve were conquered by. (See Genesis 3:1) Do you know what is the draw, the lure of the smallest, most innocent looking bait? It is the tiniest deviation from My truth for it is enough to destroy a fortress. Let me show you something."

"Now face Me."

I turn and give Him my attention.

A dark stone comes from the right, flies in between us and I turn to look at it. The space in which it flies through as well as the ground it lands upon turns dark. The light around me fades as the darkness spreads. I search for Jesus and cry out to Him. I cannot see Him or find Him. As I look all around me the darkness is eating away at my surroundings like a cancer and the light is beginning to fade. No! I cry. In the name of Jesus, No! Jesus is Lord! I close my eyes to what was happening around me and declare who Jesus is, that there is none beside Him. He alone is the truth and the righteousness! I desire You and You alone, Jesus. No one else has the words of life. I see Him come to me again as His presence lights up the darkness.

"Child, do you see how quickly one speck of doubt can destroy the light and the truth I bring into one's life? It took your focus off of Me, and then the darkness grabbed your attention. Soon fear set in and you were grappling for what bits of truth were left, but it faded in your hands. At that point many just submit to the darkness and let it take over without a fight. You proclaimed who I am and My promises. You clung to the truth you knew. Your declaration of truth drew you close to Me again."

"Now, let's try this again. What should you do this time?"

I should focus on You and trust You in all things.

"What must you do first?"

Lord, forgive me. Forgive me of my doubt and fear. Cleanse me from all unrighteousness. Make me holy and pure before You through Your blood and sacrifice. You promised in Your Word that when we turn to You, repent and confess our sins, You are faithful and just to forgive us our sins and cleanse us from all unrighteousness. (See I John 1:7-10)

Once again Jesus touches my shoulder for a moment. His light fills me and spreads all around me to light up everything surrounding me. I look at all that is around me and recognize them again as different aspects, events, people and moments in my life. I turn to face my Lord. Jesus, help me to stay focused on You. Increase my faith. Just as He smiles a rock flies past me. I see the dark trail before my eyes. This time, though, I take a step closer to Jesus.

You promised Lord to be my fortress and to be my protector from the enemy. I ask You to deliver me from the enemy. (See Psalm 18:1-3)

I fight hard to not look at the rock or at the darkness that I know is surrounding my feet. I take another step towards Him. I watch Jesus take a step away from me. Fighting the doubt and fear that is trying to overtake me, I focus intently at His face. He reaches His hands out and takes another step away. I can sense the darkness swirling up trying to wrap around me.

Jesus, You are Lord of heaven and earth! All that is seen and unseen was created by Your word. I am fearfully and wonderfully made by You and my Father in heaven who is the God Most High! I stand solely on Your promises and on Your faithfulness! I love You. I choose You!

I keep walking towards Jesus. He continues to step backwards, one step at a time, away from me. I fight to stay focused on Him. I keep walking closer and closer to Him. I know, He will never leave me, nor forsake me. I feel like a young child learning to walk and her daddy is stepping backwards encouraging her to keep going. You alone are worthy of all honor and glory. You alone are holy, righteous and true. You alone are worthy of my love, devotion and attention.

I feel the darkness grow and wrap around me. I refuse to let it have me. I start to run to Jesus, the One who lived and died for me to redeem me with His own blood. I will trust You, Lord. I run and fight to reach His extended arms. He smiles, stops and lets me run into His arms. His glory wraps around me and destroys any darkness that tried to take hold of me.

"Well done, child. Not only can doubt grow and destroy, it will pursue. You resisted the lie, denying its power. Even though it appeared to be all around you, you knew the truth and My truth set you free, did it not?"

Yes, Lord. You alone have the power to defeat the enemy. Where else can I run? Help me, Lord, to remember the power of doubt. Help me to immediately recognize the lie and speak aloud Your truth. Help me to remember that sometimes I have to fight for You and run to You and seek You with my whole heart. It does not mean You are not with me, but that You desire me to have the victory in You over the enemy. Thank you for training me to be stronger, wiser and more faithful to You; to love You with my whole heart, soul, mind and strength.

"Do not doubt, child. Do not doubt when the world tells you a lie about Me or you. Do not believe the lies when the enemy speaks to you. Proclaim My truth and My Word. Proclaim My love for you."

Thank you, my Lord. Thank you.

"Do not doubt. Do not let anyone or anything steal the truth I have placed within you. Protect it, cherish it, do not throw it away or discard it. Do not drop it or let go in any way."

Lord, I noticed I was to fight for you when doubt enters near. Why not rebuke it?

"Remember Eve? She walked and talked with Me. She knew Me and My word. The moment she turned her focus upon the enemy and his lie, doubt entered her. You cannot fight doubt with anything but Me and My truth. Resist the temptation to look upon the doubt, for it is a lie. The more you resist the doubt and stand upon My truth, the stronger your foundation will become and the easier it will be to stand the next time."

Dialogue 12

Loving God for Who He Is

"We are of God. He who knows God listens to us. He who is not of God doesn't listen to us. By this we know the spirit of truth, and the spirit of error. Beloved, let us love one another, for love is of God; and everyone who loves has been born of God, and knows God. He who doesn't love doesn't know God, for God is love. By this God's love was revealed in us, that God has sent his one and only Son into the world that we might live through him. In this is love, not that we loved God, but that he loved us, and sent his Son as the atoning sacrifice for our sins. Beloved, if God loved us in this way, we also ought to love one another. No one has seen God at any time. If we love one another, God remains in us, and his love has been perfected in us." - I John 4:6-12 (WEB)

The Anticipation

"He who doesn't love doesn't know God, for God is love." - I John 4:8 (WEB)

How do you define love? After you have written your answer below then look at I Corinthians 13:4-13 for a biblical definition. How did you do?

John 15:13 (WEB) says, *"Greater love has no one than this, that someone lay down his life for his friends."* Jesus died on the cross for our sins. He laid his life down for you. In effect Jesus has called you His friend. You can't earn that! Friendship is something that is freely given and received between two individuals. You can sell your possessions, feed the poor and join a church and basically be a good person by the world's standards. But if you say, "No" to Jesus, then you say "No" to the offer of friendship. If you reject the offer of friendship that He has given you then where else are you going to go to be a friend of God. What else can you do but say, "Yes" to Jesus? Today would you ask Jesus to be your friend?

The Conversation

Lord, you have shown me great and marvelous things. What would You have me write for this book?

"What have you learned from Me, child?"

So much, Lord, I cannot remember all the glorious and marvelous things you have taught me. Please bring them to remembrance for me.

He smiles. "Search the Scriptures. Every word is from Me. My faithful ones have written down My words as I would have them. Each word is truth and proclaims My nature and character. Truth is completed in Me for there is no other standard to which truth can be compared."

"Love. All that is lovely and pure comes from Me. One cannot know true love except through Me. True love is sacrificial love. It gives of itself for truth and truth alone. I demonstrated the standard for love in My life, death and resurrection. Love is the source of power unimaginable to man. For by it the victory over death, sin and the evil one was accomplished. Love has to be chosen of free will. Not only given, but received. There can be no force, no demands placed upon it, only an open hand with the free gift extended to be received the same way. This is the greatest crown one can have in one's life. Yes, the crown of love from My hand is eternal life."

"There is much you learned about love. You have experienced what My love is not as well as what My love is. The love I offer to man has been polluted with man's understanding. Not only is it polluted in teaching but also in receiving. Man seems to think he knows what he wants. How can he know if he does not know where he came from? How is a boy to know he is the prince of the land unless someone tells him the truth. Then, does he naturally know what that means? No. He must first become the prince, live as the prince, experience and know the court, the love of his father and mother and all the spheres of understanding of being a prince."

"Many teachers speak of what they do not know. The people receive what is taught with their own darkened hearts lacking wisdom and under-standing." As He finishes speaking, I ponder on His words and begin to realize the depth of the truth He is teaching.

Dialogue 13

Perspective of the King

"Jesus therefore said to those Jews who had believed him, 'If you remain in my word, then you are truly my disciples. You will know the truth, and the truth will make you free.'" - John 8:31, 32 (WEB)

The Anticipation

"And You will know the truth, and the truth will make you free." - John 8:32 (WEB)

In Isaiah 55:8, God declares that His thoughts are not our thoughts, and that His ways are not our ways. Some people think because they can't understand God, that they can't have a relationship with Him. Others take comfort in the knowledge that God isn't like man and feel drawn to Him. How can knowing that God is different cause you to feel separated from God and in what ways does it draw you closer?

Just a few verses earlier in Isaiah 55:6 (WEB), the prophet Isaiah writes, *"Seek Yahweh while he may be found. Call on him while he is near."* We can seek the Lord in the Scripture. The Bible is the true source of our truth. Nothing rivals it when it comes to knowing the truth about God, but you must choose to seek out that truth. Today I encourage you to read John chapter 1 and answer these questions:

1. Who created mankind? (See John 1:3)

2. On whose name do you get the right to become a Child of God? (See John 1:12)

3. Who brings grace and truth? (See John 1:14)

4. Who came to take away the sins of the world? (See John 1:29)

Don't let a lack of understanding keep you from knowing Jesus. Your future according to the Scripture is found only in Jesus, He is the only way. (See John 14:6) As for your thoughts, think on this: have you acknowledged Him? Close by reading Romans 10:8-10.

The Conversation

You alone are the Most High God. I surrender all I am to You for Your glory and honor. I feel His hands placed on top of mine. Write Lord, I am only an instrument in your hands.

"Do you trust Me?" Yes, Lord. I still ask You to increase my faith. Increase in me, Lord Jesus, so I may decrease even more.

"Come with Me." I follow where He leads. I am led to a very dark alley in a large city. There is much going on all around me including people coming and going, some standing, others sitting. It is filthy and stifling as I look at the doors leading into the tall buildings surrounding us.

"Look at Me, Child." I look up at my Lord. He is radiant and bright, shining as the stars with a white that is clean and perfect. I have never seen anything on earth in comparison to His brilliance.

"Whose eyes?"

What do You mean?

"Whose eyes can see the truth?" He asks and turns to look at the people.

I also look at them. Only Yours Lord, for you see from every angle, from every situation, from every perspective. Only You can see the truth.

"Good, My child. Remember that. Not only as I teach you, but also as you walk in the world. Even if one man can speak a word that may include My truth, it is only a speck, a corner, a fragment of My truth. Now look."

He lets me see through something before me, like glasses or binoculars. I peer through them to the people on the street. How can I describe what I see? In a moment, I see not only their lives but their hearts. I see their past, present and future, not only how they connect with the person who stands near them, but also with the situations, environments, and influences that touch them. The view is not two dimensional or even three dimensional, but all wrapped or folded within each other, separate and still corporately intertwined. My mind cannot comprehend the totality of what He shows me. It is enough for me, though, to grasp the fact that God knows every detail that has any influence, impact, or connection to every moment in time in relationship to any one person at any given moment. Not only that, but He knows the heart of each individual intimately, regardless if the person acknowledges Him or not.

"No one can comprehend My ways, My perspective or My will. I am with the Father. We are One in complete unity and harmony, in control of all that exists. Yet, we have given the right to man to choose for himself his eternal destiny. Man is unique from all of creation. Man alone was formed by My hand and created in My image. I breathed My breath into him. Man alone has been purchased by My blood. Man alone will know the joy of My love for all eternity as a choice of redemption. Even though there are questions unanswered in the lives of man, I alone have the understanding and the perspective from eternity. There are many who hear Me, yet they all do not acknowledge it is Me they hear. The deceptions are strong including the lies that come from the enemy, the world, and others."

Dialogue 14

What is Truth?

Pilate therefore said to him, "Are you a king then?"

Jesus answered, "You say that I am a king. For this reason I have been born, and for this reason I have come into the world, that I should testify to the truth. Everyone who is of the truth listens to my voice."

Pilate said to him, "What is truth?"

When he had said this, he went out again to the Jews, and said to them, "I find no basis for a charge against him." - John 18:37, 38 (WEB)

The Anticipation

Pilate said to him, "What is truth?" - John 18:38(a) (WEB)

Pilate could not hear the truth because of his perceptions of reality, so he asked the question, "What is truth?" Have you ever given thought to that question? How would you define truth? Ask 100 people and you would probably get 100 different answers. Some people think there is no such thing as absolute truth. As Christians we believe that absolute truth exists and that it can only be found in God's Word. Do you think absolute truth exists? Why or why not?

Everyone has a worldview. A worldview is how you perceive the world around you. It is the perception that people develop based on their understanding of things which they have been taught or experienced. In what ways can a man's view hinder his ability to read Scripture?

The Bible says that all Scripture is given by the inspiration of God, and is profitable for doctrine, for reproof, for correction, and for instruction in righteousness. If you find yourself glossing over or dismissing any part of Scripture, then step back and reexamine your views. This may be an indicator that you need to dig deeper with the intentional decision that you may have to let go of some aspect of your understanding. Today ask God's Holy Spirit to reveal to you in the Scripture His truth. Let Him know you desire His truth only. (See John 14:26 & II Timothy 3:16)

The Conversation

"My words are eternal. They shall never be blotted out or removed. For what I have spoken is evidenced within all realms of eternity. Not one word of Mine is lost, not one word spoken frivolously, not one word will return void of its intent and purpose."

Father, what about when we read Your word and it appears that You have changed Your mind, like the establishment of the New Covenant (Jeremiah 31:31-34) or when it appears that you have rescinded a promise?

"My purpose will be achieved to its fullness regardless of the workings or decisions of man. My way is perfect, right and just, filled with mercy and love. The enemy uses man to try to destroy or invalidate even one word of Mine. He is the destroyer and murderer from the beginning. Man does not typically consider, much less understand, My eternal nature in his equation when trying to grasp My ways."

I see, our understanding of the intent of Your words, do not in any way affect Your words or purpose. What we may see from our clouded view of You and Your words is not the fullness of Your truth. From our perspective of a situation along with our interpretation and reasoning, we may think You are illogical, contradictory or even wrong. Forgive us Lord for our unbelief. Have mercy and compassion on us. Help us to understand Your ways to the fullness as You have created us.

"Man cannot understand that which is beyond his scope of knowledge. Even when men come together to view in greater detail, rarely are they seeking the truth because of the desires of their heart to be greater than I have created them to be. Their pride greatly influences their perspective. Remember the Tower of Babel? If you look with open eyes, you will see men once again building a tower to their own conclusion of their pride and arrogance. Just a small piece of truth they have stolen, to design a greater evil, to destroy and murder. Blood shall be required from all who stand against Me. Even more than blood, their very souls shall be required."

Lord Jesus, my Messiah. I stand in awe of You and Your greatness. Every day I learn more and more of You, of Your nature and Your truth. I wonder how I can receive Your blessings and Your Spirit with the gratitude and fullness as You deserve. Help me with this Lord. You said before You can only teach or reveal what is within one's doctrine or understanding. I do not want to be like that. I want to be open to all You desire to teach and reveal to me. I know Your understanding is much higher than mine. I ask for the wisdom and understanding to perceive and process correctly what You are sharing with me. Let me not distort or twist or misconstrue Your truth in order to meet my preconceived ideas, doctrine, understanding or philosophies. I know that You will be in total accordance with Your Word, not my or any man's understanding of Your Scriptures, but with Your truth of Your Scriptures. I realize how limited man is and how quick we tend to conform Your Word and truth to our desires and agenda. I praise You for Your ultimate wisdom in that all Scripture is perfect. We, in our limited understanding of the mysteries of the One True God, cannot dismiss even one word in Your Scripture. Your truth, Your view of Your truth is what I desire. I trust You!

Dialogue 15

Follow Jesus Home

"Seek Yahweh while he may be found. Call on him while he is near. Let the wicked forsake his way, and the unrighteous man his thoughts. Let him return to Yahweh, and he will have mercy on him; and to our God, for he will freely pardon. 'For my thoughts are not your thoughts, and your ways are not my ways,' says Yahweh. 'For as the heavens are higher than the earth, so are my ways higher than your ways, and my thoughts than your thoughts.' "- Isaiah 55:6-9 (WEB)

The Anticipation

"For my thoughts are not your thoughts, and your ways are not my ways," says Yahweh." - Isaiah 55:8 (WEB)

Consider the path you are currently on. Would you like to see a change of direction? Or even a completely different path? In what way?

In order to follow God on His path, you have to be willing to course correct which may including acknowledging you have made wrong decisions. Are you willing to submit to Jesus' authority and wisdom to allow Him to direct your ways? In what areas do you struggle in surrender?

The Conversation

I walk towards the Lord Jesus. Oh, how I praise Your name and desire to declare of Your goodness! Your mercies truly endure forever! Lord, this is Your book. I only want Your truth to be upon these pages.

As I walk beside Jesus, I realize I am looking up at Him like I am a child. His beauty and glory is indescribable, beyond all understanding. I realize what I perceive is only a glimpse of His true being and glory. There is nothing more beautiful in all creation in comparison to the Lord Jesus, even in the limited view I have of His presence. His smile alone has the power to melt any fear, any doubt, and any discouragement away. To stand before Him as His eyes look upon me is to stand in the midst of an overwhelming love. His love is as a consuming fire of such intensity one cannot stand. The only reason I do not fall is because He Himself upholds me. Oh, yes, every knee shall bow and every tongue shall confess Jesus is Lord!

"You know enough of My nature now to be able to discern truth from a lie. Why is it difficult to walk on the path of righteousness?" (See Romans 7:14-20)

He leads me to a great garden that was not made by human hands. All is perfectly in place while being as natural looking as a meadow that spans for miles. Jesus sits down on a marble bench. He lifts me up to sit beside Him to look at the beautiful expanse around us. The birds are singing in a harmonious chorus like I have never heard before as the spectacular butterflies flitter from flower to flower. The colors are vibrant and fresh.

Well, I am not sure Lord. I know sometimes I just can't see a path or somehow find myself wandering off. I look up at His gentle face. Tell me. Tell me of Your path and how I can walk safely in Your will.

"Look, child, look at all you see around you."

I stand up on the bench and look around me. I see rolling hills as far as the eye can see. Everything is beyond beauty and life abundant. I notice one dark area in the trees. My eye keeps going there, like I am wanting to know what it is.

"Ah. What if I told you, you could explore all you see, but to not go near the darkness?"

I look sheepishly at Him. I knew the truth in my heart and I knew He knew. Sooner or later, I would be drawn to that area to peer in. I would finally get enough confidence to take a few steps in to see what I could see. And, yes, I acknowledge that I would get lost in the darkness. Lord, even if I told You I know that I would get lost and it is dangerous in there, I know I would still end up in there. It is drawing me, pulling at me, as if it has a grip over me that I cannot deny.

"And yet you know you could explore for an eternity in this garden and that darkness will call you and eventually take you in."

Yes, I know. Why Lord? Why are we like this? Why are we weak and taken over by darkness so easily? I know the only way I could stay away is if You were here with me. You would keep me safe. You would remind me of the truth which would help me overcome the temptation of the darkness. Your presence alone would be enough for me to flee from it.

He waves His hand before me over the dark area. As He did so, the darkness fades away. I can see clearly beyond the trees and I saw a dark large pit that leads to depths far from God. Now that I know the truth, I won't go near there.

"Why was My command for you not good enough beforehand?"

I slump beside Him. "Lord, You know."

"Yes. I know. I created man with the will to choose. I placed My law in every heart along with the understanding of right and wrong. This is important. You knew the truth about that dark area. You knew it was dangerous and you should not go. Yet, you were drawn to it. That is the trap. Where was your focus? You said if I was with you, you would not go there, but in your own strength with no help, you would. You see, man cannot obey the truth I have placed in his heart. That law creates a battle within a person. Some have chosen Me through faith such as the saints of old. But many did not desire the truth and rejected it. Then I came to set the captives free, to proclaim the good news of the Kingdom of God. My death and resurrection breaks that bondage, that lure or call of the trap that leads to hell."

Jesus holds my hand in His. "Now, I am walking with you. I walk with all who call upon Me, surrender themselves to my Lordship, and who repent of their ways to follow Mine. I will lead them home safely to the arms of their eternal Father."

We stand and start to walk. As we walk, a path appears under each of His footsteps! The path is just big enough to allow me to walk on it beside Jesus and far enough before us to light the next step. It is brilliant clear golden in color and radiates light from His footsteps. He stops. I am about to take another step and notice the path stops with Him. If I take another step, I will be off the path. I realize that if I am not holding His hand tightly I would keep walking and step off His path completely. I notice He is holding my hand gently enough to let it slide out if I want to continue. It is my grip on Him that stops me.

I look up at Him and step back. I am sorry, Lord. I was not paying attention to You.

He smiles and we continue on our way. He shows me flowers, insects, animals and the trees. I marvel at all the beauty around me. I continue in awe at the creation of the translucent path with every footstep He takes. The path is still visible behind us as we travel.

I let go and run off to a patch of very large berries. He was close with me and I knew I was safe. Immediately briars surround me and the thorns start to cut into my skin. I look around in horror. The briars continue to raise above my head as darkness closes in. I cry out for Jesus. He has to be near, He was right there!

Lord, where are You?

"I am right here. I am always with you, I will never leave you," He says calmly.

It is so dark and it is painful here. You seem so far away.

"You ran off. This was not where you were to go. You not only stepped off the path, but you also pulled away from Me."

I am sorry, Lord. I knew He was right. I understood. I had taken my eyes off of Him and the path He was preparing for me. I also forgot His hand, His perfect, strong and powerful hand that was also gentle and loving. How could I run off from what He had prepared for me and desire something else? Somehow I realize that if He wanted me to have the berries, He would have brought me here safely, in His timing. Forgive me, Lord. I know Your way is better than my way. You know everything including what is best for me. Help me.

I surrender myself to Jesus and His will. He wraps His cloak around me and fills me with His light. He gently restores me to the place beside Him on the path. I feel a bit awkward at first, even unsteady on my feet as I stand on His path. Then I raise my hand to reach for His. He gives me such a sweet smile that I am filled with tremendous joy. We continue to walk together. This time, I stay focused on Him and His words. I pay such close attention to every aspect of Him I can: His face, His feet, the warmth that flows through His hand into mine. How can I ever take my focus off of Him? I know the safest, most blessed place to be in all creation, is right here, walking beside the Lord of Heaven and Earth who loves me more than I can comprehend. (See I John 1:9, 10)

Thank you, Jesus. You are precious to me.

"Life is a journey, child. So much around you seems harmless, even good. The truth is, anything that is not of My will for you can be harmful or dangerous for you. Stay with Me. Obey Me. Seek Me and learn from Me. Remember, I love you and desire to bring you safely home to Your Father in Heaven who loves you more than all the stars in the sky."

He crouches down a bit like an adult would to talk to a child face to face. He smiles and says with such love that fills me with hope beyond measure, "In eternity with Us, there is nothing contrary to Our nature. There is no darkness, no lies, no traps, no pain, no death. There is only Our glory with which you will have full communion for all eternity! Follow Me home, My precious child. Follow Me home."

He stands up as He holds my gaze. Holding my hand gently in His firm hand, we turn and walk on.

Dialogue 16

Jesus' Journey

"When I consider your heavens, the work of your fingers, the moon and the stars, which you have ordained; what is man, that you think of him? What is the son of man, that you care for him? For you have made him a little lower than God, and crowned him with glory and honor. You make him ruler over the works of your hands. You have put all things under his feet: All sheep and cattle, yes, and the animals of the field, the birds of the sky, the fish of the sea, and whatever passes through the paths of the seas. Yahweh, our Lord, how majestic is your name in all the earth!" - Psalm 8:3-9 (WEB)

The Anticipation

"You make him ruler over the works of your hands. You have put all things under his feet" - Psalm 8:6 (WEB)

We are to consider the heavens, the work of His fingers. But what of His feet, the road He has traveled? Have you considered the steps God has taken, the choices He has made just so He can be with you and you with Him? If you haven't given it much thought, do so now.

When you consider the roads you have traveled, are you amazed that God desires to walk with you, that he longs for your footprints to join His? What effect have the footsteps of Jesus had on your life?

The Psalmist ends His writings declaring the excellence of God's name in all the earth. How can you praise God today? Take a moment to give honor and glory to Jesus.

The Conversation

I stop to praise God for my heart is filled with joy and hope because of Him. He meets me in the garden and sits me down before Him on a marble bench.

"Sing to Me," He says. I start to think of 'Glorious Day' by Casting Crowns, but the words are not coming to my mind. I look at Jesus; He smiles and says, "Songs are not always with words, child."

I close my eyes and quiet my heart. I am a bit startled as a song rises from within me to the King of Kings. There are no words, not even a distinguishable note of music to my ear, just a song of love flowing from my heart and spirit.

As I rejoice before Him, I look down at His beautiful feet and I see them on a gold path, different in perspective than the one we walk on. The path has within it the journey His feet had traveled. I see His feet as He stood in His Glory in Heaven from the beginning of time. Then He steps out of eternity to become Emmanuel, God With Us. My heart nearly explodes as I see His tiny feet being caressed in His mother's hand. Next, they become toddler feet taking unsteady steps as they transition into the playful feet of a young child. Then they transition to adolescent feet walking on a dusty road becoming the tough, sandaled feet of a man. The feet stop as knees fall into the form of a praying man. Ever so quickly they twist in anguish with the sound of whips and screams. Standing, they appear heavy laden, with blood dripping down mixing with the dust on the road. Then they lay down with nails being impaled in them. With my heart heavy, I see only His feet as He is wrapped in cloth and laid in the tomb. But then, with an explosion of light, His radiant feet walk from the tomb with power and authority displaying as they step back into Heaven! And now, those feet are walking on a path of brilliant gold beside mine.

Oh, to sing a thousand songs to the One who has walked a journey like no other; a journey of love that goes beyond anything we can comprehend. He has a love for every person He has ever created or will create, even while they were filled with sin and a hatred for Him. A love that will find fullness and remain forever for those who choose to receive Him as their Lord and Savior.

Dialogue 17

The Source of One's Truth

"For I am not ashamed of the Good News of Christ, for it is the power of God for salvation for everyone who believes; for the Jew first, and also for the Greek. For in it is revealed God's righteousness from faith to faith. As it is written, "But the righteous shall live by faith." For the wrath of God is revealed from heaven against all ungodliness and unrighteousness of men, who suppress the truth in unrighteousness, because that which is known of God is revealed in them, for God revealed it to them. For the invisible things of him since the creation of the world are clearly seen, being perceived through the things that are made, even his everlasting power and divinity; that they may be without excuse. Because, knowing God, they didn't glorify him as God, neither gave thanks, but became vain in their reasoning, and their senseless heart was darkened." - Romans 1:16-21 (WEB)

The Anticipation

"For the invisible things of him since the creation of the world are clearly seen, being perceived through the things that are made, even his everlasting power and divinity; that they may be without excuse." - Romans 1:20 (WEB)

The Apostle Paul makes a case that a visible universe testifies to an invisible God and the attributes of that universe testify of God's power and ability. Yet people still turn away from what they can see in a vibrant living universe and worship things made of stone and wood leaving them without excuse. When people deny there is a creator behind the wonder they see, they begin to believe lies and this causes men's hearts to be darkened. In what ways do you see mankind deny God and how does that denial impact our world? What can you learn about God the creator by simply observing His handiwork?

The Scripture teaches us in I Chronicles 29 that everything we need comes from God and that we can only give what He first gave us. Ask God in prayer to provide what you need this week. While you're at it, take time to give thanks for what you do have.

The Conversation

Jesus leads me to a porch step. We sit down together and before us is the expanse of the universe. The steps stop so that all that is around us, under us and above us is the vastness and beauty of space. I feel safe sitting next to Jesus as I quietly wait for Him.

"Do you see all that I created for man to explore and enjoy?"

I smile, as I look around. I know there is even a greater expanse beyond what we can see.

Jesus reaches His hand out and brings into closer view a planet I do not recognize. It is before us spinning slowly as He says, "You have heard of Alpha Centauri?"

I have heard the name, but I know nothing of it.

"The planet there was created far away from earth to be found by man. It is nothing like the earth. We wanted man to know that of all the billions of planets, only one was perfectly designed and created just for him. None other in all the universe is suitable, fit for life."

Now He holds in His hand Earth as it rotates in His palm. "Only one has everything man needs to live, thrive, and work. Everything he ever needed is right here." He leans back and looks at me. "Why do you think man looks outside of what has already been provided for him?"

That is a good question and I considered possible answers. We always want more than what we have, never satisfied, always seeking and desiring more.

"Yes child, but there is another desire at work. Come with Me. You have questions about the universe and want to see it closer."

I nod and ask Him about black holes. He brings one before us and says, "Everything came from nothing. So everything can go back to nothing."

Why destroy what you created Lord?

"So man would know We have the power to create and the power to destroy." I see flashes of creation and destruction. Each image is very fast and I cannot distinguish them individually. I hear sounds and feel the impact of what He is showing me. "Everything was created so man would know We are God. Man always desires more because man was created that way."

So we can desire more of you?

Jesus said, "Yes child. All of creation, the heavens above and everything seen on earth displays Our immutable and perfect nature."

I am stuck Lord. "Nature" is a word that I struggle with right now to fit You. Our words are not only limited, but can be easily twisted out of truth and into mistruth. You are greater and higher than any aspect of understanding. I am seeing as I write how even Your own words in the Bible can be received by the minds and hearts of people as ideas that are not Yours. So many refuse to accept Your truth as You intend it, so they change it to fit their own doctrine.

"Thus all the Scriptures about My truth being hidden from the hearts and minds of man, the need for parables, and verses about the hope that is within each person to know My truth. The difference in the hearts of men is their desire for either My truth or for their truths that they can twist and contort to seemingly fit My words."

Lord, what puzzles me is that men will fight for their own desires and form of truth they want so badly that they will twist Your words to fit their own agenda. And yet, You know all, You know the hearts of men, You know their very thoughts. When they stand before You one day, they will be not only accountable for their own thoughts and desires and personal sin against You, they will be accountable for every word spoken, every person they led astray, every soul they kept from You and Your truth. My heart breaks for them, wanting them to know what they are doing so they would surrender their truths to receive Yours as You intend.

As I am ready to ask God to somehow tell them and convict them, I realize He already did. There are so many verses in the Bible proclaiming God's warnings of this very thing. I see many of the verses and parables flash through my mind. Then, the final verses I see are written before me as if in bold and capital letters, Romans 1:18-32. Keep me, Lord, near You, humble and always desiring Your truth as You are the 'I AM' in whom all truth and good resides.

Dialogue 18

Unity in Christ

"I therefore, the prisoner in the Lord, beg you to walk worthily of the calling with which you were called, with all lowliness and humility, with patience, bearing with one another in love; being eager to keep the unity of the Spirit in the bond of peace. There is one body, and one Spirit, even as you also were called in one hope of your calling; one Lord, one faith, one baptism, one God and Father of all, who is over all, and through all, and in us all." - Ephesians 4:1-6 (WEB)

The Anticipation

"...being eager to keep the unity of the Spirit in the bond of peace." - Ephesians 4:3 (WEB)

To walk with the Lord is to walk in unity with Him and with others. What are some of the obstacles that you face that hinder your ability to walk in unity with God? With others?

Have you ever considered how our views and even religious teachings separate and divide us as Christians? How can they impact our effectiveness in the world as Christians?

What about you, do you desire more of Jesus? Do you desire His truth more than you desire to be right? Pray about how you can have a closer walk with God and others.

The Conversation

"What would you do if you had more of Me?"

I am not sure, only You know Lord. When there have been times I have experienced more of You, then I desire to be even closer to You. There are times though when You withdraw for whatever reason, or maybe when I withdraw because of the busyness or struggles in life. Then I settle for other things because I feel like I am unworthy to receive more of You. If only I would keep on seeking You, regardless.

"Imagine a hundred people in unity seeking Me."

I cannot imagine it. We are so fractured and in disunity. It is hard for me to comprehend so many people in complete unity. My Lord, You are greater than we are, I know anything is possible with You. You said in Your Word that You only needed two or three to be together. Tell me, how can we truly be in unity together?

"Even with your body, when one part is hurt, the rest cares for and protects the weak part. Yet, the body keeps working, moving forward, doing what it needs to. My people need to be in unity, through Me and My Spirit just as the physical body works together. Then you will be able to take care of each other, regardless of any obstacle."

The prophet Isaiah said that when You reign Lord in righteousness, then our rulers will make wise decisions and the people will be safe, the heart of rash men will give way to understanding, and we will be unified then. Why are we not seeing more of that now?

"Remember, people will only receive from Me what fits into their doctrine or understanding of Me and My word."

But Lord, You have set people free even from their doctrine, including me. So many examples are in Scriptures, including Paul who wrote much of the New Testament. I also remember how You worked with my friend with his doctrinal views.

"Yes, but they desired My truth more than they desired their doctrine."

Can You teach us how to help Your people have that same hunger and thirst for Your truth over their own doctrine? Or is this something we pray for and ask for Your help?

"Find where the unity or agreement is in My truth and build from there. Praise Me together. Yes, use intercessory prayer and pray together. Bear with each other, love each other, have mercy, and always forgive. You can challenge each other in love."

Is there a way to be in unity with others around the world who are Your remnant? How can we encourage, love and empower those in other countries? I begin to see silver threads joining together and interconnecting with the Lord. I begin to understand in a new sense how all Christians are connected not only to God through His Spirit, but also to each other. Can I pray for them? (See John 17)

"Your prayers transcend time and space."

My heart fills as I begin to pray earnestly for my brothers and sisters in Christ whom I have never met. As I pray, I can feel the power of the Lord in each word. Remind me, Lord, to remember Your Church in prayer.

Dialogue 19

God's Indestructible Truth

"For to this end the Good News was preached even to the dead, that they might be judged indeed as men in the flesh, but live as to God in the spirit. But the end of all things is near. Therefore be of sound mind, self-controlled, and sober in prayer. And above all things be earnest in your love among yourselves, for love covers a multitude of sins. Be hospitable to one another without grumbling. As each has received a gift, employ it in serving one another, as good managers of the grace of God in its various forms." - I Peter 4:6-10 (WEB)

The Anticipation

"And above all things be earnest in your love among yourselves, for love covers a multitude of sins." - I Peter 4:8 (WEB)

Love covers a multitude of sins. Let me give you an imperfect illustration of what this means. Even though someone you love does something that bothers you, you tend to overlook it, especially when your heart is filled with compassion and joy. But when you are hurt, jealous or angry, then your love can become cold. Now all you can see are their faults and sins.

Now read John 17:23. Have you considered the truth of this passage? What does it mean to you that God loves you like He loves Jesus? What are the implications for you? How is God's love for you covering your sins? What role does this play in your forgiveness?

Do you struggle believing that this love of God can be true? And yet we know that God doesn't lie, His words are true (See II Samuel 7:28). If God does not lie, then God really does love you like that! How will you respond to His love? Today give thanks to God for His love. Love him back. One way you can do that is by loving others. Who has sinned against you that you need to cover with your love, like God has covered you? Don't try to be perfect, just love and be loved.

The Conversation

Lord Jesus, You alone are God with our Father, The Most High God. I know no other who is like you. You alone hold all power, all truth, all good, and all that is right. To You alone is all honor, glory and praise due. How I desire to know the depth, the width, the breadth of Your love and truth! Each word in Scripture holds eternity within, how can we grasp anything of Your majesty? Speak, Lord, your servant is waiting.

"Remember, perfection is not to be achieved at all costs. Love though, love is desired above all. Love covers a multitude of sins. My love for you is seen in My Son. As I encompass and surround Him, so I do you. Nothing is greater than love, nothing more powerful, nothing else is eternal. It comes from Me, and it will return to Me."

I see what appears to be water flowing from God to the earth. Not one drop of the water is wasted. Every drop of water is accounted for as it returns back to Heaven. I never thought of that before Lord, everything that flows from You, will return to You.

"Not one word of Mine will return void, and not one jot or tittle will be lost. It is not up to men to take from Me and destroy. They do not have that power. A Bible may be burned, but that only brings the words of its judgment unto them. Destroying it cannot touch or stain or remove or even smear the truth it contains. My words have been spoken. They shall be accomplished in their fullness regardless of anything or anyone else."

Father's words still resound in thunder with His power amplifying the truth He speaks.

"What does that mean to you child?"

I am just trying to soak in the immense truth that I just heard. Every person, as well as everything in creation, has been created by and for and through Your word. Scriptures are flowing through us, Jesus is the light, and this light is God with us. I am understanding a greater depth of how Jesus fulfilled the Law. The new covenant is why we become a new creation when we are saved. It is like doors of understanding are opening up inside me.

"What you have known as teaching and truth from men, let go. They see through a glass darkly. Think about the church lesson you taught today. The author of that lesson shared a segment of truth I have revealed to him but he did not and could not receive the depth and magnitude of My truth. What is it you want? Deep in your heart, look for it, seek for it. What is it?" (See John 14:26)

Help me Lord. Walk with me and reveal to me the desire of my heart. Jesus stands as if at the edge of my heart, my very being. Somehow I understand He is going to reveal to me my innermost self. I am fearful, for I know my past. Jesus walks beside me. What I expect to be darkness inside, is actually clean and bright. I look up at Jesus.

He smiles back, "I did this. You let Me come here. You prayed for forgiveness, I gave it to you. You asked to be cleansed, I cleansed you. You desired Me, I filled you." (I John 1:9)

His light and glory shines from Him and fills the area in which we are standing. I receive Him and His glory. More, Lord, More! I want More of You, Jesus, and less of me!

Dialogue 20

Giver of All That is Good

"Ask, and it will be given you. Seek, and you will find. Knock, and it will be opened for you. For everyone who asks receives. He who seeks finds. To him who knocks it will be opened. Or who is there among you, who, if his son asks him for bread, will give him a stone? Or if he asks for a fish, who will give him a serpent? If you then, being evil, know how to give good gifts to your children, how much more will your Father who is in heaven give good things to those who ask him!" - Matthew 7:7-11 (WEB)

The Anticipation

"Ask, and it will be given you. Seek, and you will find. Knock, and it will be opened for you." - Matthew 7:7 (WEB)

Ask and it will be given to you. This idea is echoed in Mark 11:24 where it says, *"Therefore I say to you, whatever things you ask when you pray, believe that you receive them, and you will have them."* Have you ever stopped to consider the implications of this teaching? Do you have limits on what you ask for? Do you stop short of asking God for things? Are there things in your life that you haven't brought to God? Examine your prayer life now. What has prevented you from asking Him for assistance? Do you think God is too busy for you? Know this, God loves to give good things to those who ask Him. (Review the following verses: I John 3:22, & 5:14, 15)

Philippians 4:6 (WEB) says, *"In nothing be anxious, but in everything, by prayer and petition with thanksgiving, let your requests be made known to God."* What things have you been worried about? What is keeping you from praying about them now? Try listing some of the things that you need to bring to God but haven't? Next, look at Ephesians 3:20.

The Conversation

"Remember when we walked inside your life to see all was clean, bright and reflecting my Light?"

Yes, Lord, I do. My hearts sings at Your work within me! This is nothing I could have done on my own. Your promises are true to a depth I am only beginning to understand.

Next, I see before us a woman asking Jesus to come and help her fix her kitchen cabinets. He looks around at the old kitchen in desperate need of repair. Not only are the cabinets barely holding together, but the appliances are obviously rundown. The stove has only two working burners as the faucet drips its own rhythmic beat.

As Jesus walks across the patchy linoleum floor He asks her, "Is there anything else I can do for you?"

"No," she says, "Just fix these two cabinets. That is all. I do not want to bother You for more."

He takes out tools to quickly and expertly fix the two cabinets. "Are you sure that I cannot do more for you?"

"Thank You for what You have done. Nothing more. That's all," she replies.

Jesus picks up His tools, nods to the woman and leaves.

"Do you understand what I have shown you? I can do so much more abundantly in one's life, but many only want a few simple things fixed or taken care of. They do not accept the fact that not only can I, but I desire to, change their whole life. I want to remove the old and give them the new in every area of their life. I desire to and delight in pouring blessings upon My children beyond their expectations. I am limited by their beliefs and their understanding of who I Am. I was serious in desiring to show them my love and power when I said to cast all your cares upon Me, and to be anxious for nothing, but bring everything to Me in prayer with thanksgiving. (See I Peter 5:17 and Philippians 4:6) I have no limits. I am the Alpha and the Omega; I am the Creator and Finisher of all things. (See

Revelation 22:13) I Am He who binds up and looses, I am the One who rules and judges in righteousness. (See Matthew 16:19, Psalm 72:2) I Am. (See also John 8:58) And I will do My perfect will upon men. If they desire to love Me and be loved by Me, I will love them to the depth they will allow Me. For some, a simple faith is enough. For others, they desire to go as far as I will take them. The deeper one goes with Me, the less the world will affect them. Also, the fewer friends they will have. But, they shall have greater, dearer, more precious friends than they ever imagined possible. This depth of friendship you are now experiencing, yes?"

Yes my Lord! The depth of relationships with my family and closest friends who believe in You is beyond all my expectations. How can one put into words what I know now with those I love the deepest? The fulfillment of which is even greater because I know each one shall be with me in eternity. They love You too and are growing in their love for You. My heart sings at the thought of what You are doing in our lives, Jesus. Thank You!

Dialogue 21

Trust Brings Freedom

"Cause me to hear your loving kindness in the morning, for I trust in you. Cause me to know the way in which I should walk, for I lift up my soul to you. Deliver me, Yahweh, from my enemies. I flee to you to hide me. Teach me to do your will, for you are my God. Your Spirit is good. Lead me in the land of uprightness." - Psalm 143:8-10 (WEB)

The Anticipation

"Deliver me, Yahweh, from my enemies. I flee to you to hide me." - Psalm 143: 9 (WEB)

Be honest, where have you put your trust? Is your sense of security found in your retirement plan or insurance policies? Are you trusting local authorities or your home security system to keep you safe? Jot down a few ways we protect ourselves from financial loss and personal danger. Contemplate why you have taken some of these measures to protect yourself.

Consider Psalm 23:4 (WEB) where it says, *"Even though I walk through the valley of the shadow of death, I will fear no evil, for you are with me. Your rod and your staff, they comfort me."* Why do you think the rod and staff bring comfort?

Do you think it is even possible to live a life free from fear? What would you need to have to achieve this level of confidence for yourself? In today's reading, look for the answer to that question. Then take time to pray. Ask God to show you how His rod and staff can comfort you.

The Conversation

"Let Me tell you a story. An old man is walking down a long dusty road. He is heavily laden with his wares for the market which is still a few miles away. He knows the journey is long and that he is tired and worn. He also knows he has to reach the market to provide for his loved ones and himself. As he walks along the road, he kicks at a pebble. This pebble jumps ahead then rolls into the grass."

He stops the story and looks at me, "This is the fun part."

What Lord?

"Watching you try to figure out what is going to happen and yet, you know you can't. So you struggle as you try to let yourself enjoy every word spoken by Me. You think I am going to talk about one thing, then I discuss another. Yes, presumption does get in the way of truth and enjoyment with Me, does it not?"

As I consider His words, I realize they are true. I am compelled to ask Him, Why do I do that? Most people do. Is it because of our culture? Why is it so important for us to get the punch line before it is delivered?

"Yes, it is partly because of human nature. It is also due to the desire to be in control, not to look a fool. You want to appear wise and intelligent before others, also there is the idea of being prepared. Man has this idea that if he can know what is coming ahead, he can be prepared for it. The more options that could arise mean more and more preparation. Soon the person is tied up with anxiety, worries and bound up in more ways than he knew possible. So, instead, he has actually imprisoned himself. Also, when a person lives in such a presumptuous way, he oftentimes cannot see what really is happening in his life. The truth becomes the lie."

"The person has prepared the walls of protection, provision and sense of security with his own hands against a foe that has not risen up and may never appear in the future. When the real threat comes, the person tends to be blind to it out of pride or ignorance as it invades and permeates through his life."

"Now, contrast that with the person walking alongside Me, following Me, attentive to Me, receiving My Word through the Scriptures as well as receiving wisdom and understanding through My Spirit. They look to Me for their provision, their protection, their sense of security and value in life. Nothing will come to them that they cannot handle, because they are in step with Me, the Creator of heaven and earth. I hold all authority in My hand. If I tell them to go left, they go left. If I say to go right, they go right. If I tell them to stop and wait, they wait. If I tell them to flee, they do not stop to second guess, or analyze the situation, they just flee! Do you see the freedom they have? They also are not bound or contained within a box of preconceived notions or ideas created and founded by man."

I begin to see the fullness of the bondage worry and anxiety place on us as well as the freedom we receive when we trust You with every aspect of our lives.

Dialogue 22

Foundation of Love Endures the Journey

"To you I do lift up my eyes, you who sit in the heavens. Behold, as the eyes of servants look to the hand of their master, as the eyes of a maid to the hand of her mistress; so our eyes look to Yahweh, our God, until he has mercy on us." - Psalm 123:1, 2 (WEB)

The Anticipation

"To you I do lift up my eyes, you who sit in the heavens." - Psalm 123:1 (WEB)

What are your eyes looking to? Where is your focus as you walk through the day?

Do you tend to wait for the next word spoken to you by others or do you find yourself racing ahead in presumption? What are some ways you can improve in this area?

As you read the Bible, are you able to set aside your own understandings and presumptions to let God reveal more of His truth through His Spirit? What happens when you read Scriptures that do not line up with your doctrine or beliefs?

Ask God to help you identify any beliefs you have that are not His and to replace them with His truth.

The Conversation

"Let's continue with My story. Let yourself 'be' with Me as I share the story with you. This is a story you have never heard before about a man on his journey."

I quiet my heart and try to focus on just the moment, not on what will be, could be or anything to come. Just here and now with my Lord. Help me to rest in the moment with You. Teach me to comprehend and receive what

You are giving me, not what I think You have.

"As the man watches the pebble fall out of view in the fresh green grass, he is reminded of a memory from long ago. The man stops where the pebble was lost as his mind drifts to years ago. As he peers into the blades of grass, he could see his Mama. She was so tall and strong. She was more than capable of raising his six brothers and sisters along with himself. They used to be a close family. When their dad died, they pulled closer together as his mom put Christ even more to the center of their family. Since they lived in unity, they grew strong in the Lord, leaning on Him and each other. As they grew older and moved out on their own, he remembered his mom being so joyful over the lives her children were venturing out on for they each dearly loved their Lord Jesus."

"He smiles to himself as he remembers her sweet loving face promising them her love through all eternity. A tear rolls down his face as he turns to continue his journey."

As He tells me the story, I have to stop and back myself up often to wait for His wording and not mine. This is harder than I want to admit. It is hard to wait and not to jump ahead to create my own idea for the next part of the story. I wonder how much I do this throughout the day. How many choices, words, or thoughts of mine are the result of my own understanding and experience without waiting for Him to guide, direct and advise me? Oh, to have the patience and wisdom to walk circumspectly, step by step, with my Lord. I desire to be attentive to Him, hanging on every word and thought that proceeds from His mouth, that not a word would I speak or an action would I do without Him. Seems like an impossible feat to me, but I desire it. I desire to be fully submitted to my God for His full use and accomplishment of His perfect and holy will. Lord, what next?

"Child, there is an awareness that comes with relationship. The closer the relationship, the more love and devotion you have for someone, the more attentiveness and awareness you have to that person. Remember your new baby? You were aware of each whimper and movement that your daughter made those first few weeks. Then the rest of the world and your life came into conflict with that relationship. You desired to keep with her what you had from the beginning and could experience it every once in awhile, but other priorities got in the way."

"Now, consider our relationship. Immensely different because of My nature, but you are My child just the same. When I have your full awareness and attention, we experience a oneness that cannot be triumphed. When other priorities challenge for your attention, they can break our communication. There is no other god, no other power, no other hope above Me! There is none other, not even self. You desire truth, find it in Me. You desire protection, run to Me. You desire fulfillment, security, significance, direction, peace, success, joy? You will only find these in Me and Me alone. I can and will fill to the fullness according to your faith in Me."

Lord, thank you for your patience as I learn and grow in You. Your mercy and compassion are so great, I cannot comprehend You fully. I forget too easily Your perfect nature and Your patience with me. Thank you!

"As the old man continues on his way, the wares on his back seem much heavier. He stops to readjust the weight upon his back wishing he had accepted the offer of help from his friend. Looking ahead, he starts walking again straining under the weight on his back."

"When all around becomes dark, the man finds a place to rest for the night. He is so weary and worn, he wonders how he can go any further. As he drifts off to sleep a prayer lifts off his lips and fades into the darkness."

"Child, you can see how My words come upon you with ease as you rest and trust?"

Yes, The more I realize you are around me and protecting me from the enemy, the world and even my own thoughts, yes, it is easier.

"Come, let's finish the next part of the story. Listen closely, there will be a change, see if you can discern it."

Help me to learn your truth, your word, my Lord.

"As the sun rises over the horizon and falls upon the man's face, he opens his eyes to a new reality before him."

"Ah, good, now you are eagerly awaiting, not presuming, but wondering and waiting."

I am trying, it is tough though for me. I have different options fly in front of me, but I am choosing not to grab them. I am just waiting for You.

"As the man looks around, he is confused by the lights shining brightly everywhere he looks. They are brilliant lights, but he cannot find the sources. The white light is of the purest, clearest white he has ever seen."

My mind races ahead to what I think is going to happen next. I immediately stop and back up. "I will wait Lord, I will wait."

"You saw what he saw, I gave you the picture."

Yes, was that my imagination or a picture you gave me? Up until now I will admit I was imagining your story as I would if someone was reading it to me. But when I saw the light, it was clear and vibrant, as if I was there.

"The difference? Think, look back, what is the difference?"

Actually, earlier it was like watching a movie that was black and white with about fifty percent Technicolor. Some scenes were clearer, but the outer edges faded in color. In contrast, when I saw the man's surroundings with the light, it was intense, brilliant, and clear.

"Thus, the difference you will notice when I talk versus your own thoughts. Your thoughts seem clear to you, but when compared to Mine, they are faded, jagged, not in order, or low in intensity. There is a sureness when you trust Me and My words."

"Do you trust Me."

Yes, my Lord.

"Ready for a journey?"

I quiet the callings of the world requesting my attention at this moment. I choose You, You alone, now.

My eyes open in my mind to the realm of light where we left the story with the old man. I look around and stand up in awe at the splendor of the surroundings. Rays of colored beams shine through the air and somehow reflect back within itself. An immense peace and joy fill me from within to such a point it begins to flow out of me.

"I met the man here." The Lord spoke in such a gentle manner. "I met him here and he did not refuse Me. He rejoiced in My presence. You see, he fell asleep that day and never woke up. He was one of My own. For many years he loved Me and followed Me. The love his Mama gave him and his siblings along with her intensity of loving Me gave him a foundation that would carry him the rest of his life. Truth is like that. When truth is passed on in love the roots are deeper, they are stronger, and they are filled with My Holy Spirit to create a growth that can endure the hardships of life."

"Love, My child, teach My love. Give My love. Share My love. Know My love. Breathe it in, drink it in. Fill yourself with My love so you can touch the lives of others around you with My truth empowered by My love so it can take root in their lives. Know that the world's way of giving, showing and imparting love is not My way. My way is through prayer, through seeking My counsel of loving the different people I place before you. My love is through a touch, a word, eye contact, a presence without words, a hug when focusing on Me and My love for them. When you are filled with My love, it will radiate through you to those around you. Be gentle, patient, kind, forgiving, dependable, honorable, respectful and merciful. Just like Paul said, one sows, one plants, one waters, one reaps, one disciples, but all must be done with My love."

"Do you want more?"

Yes, I want more.

"When is enough, Child?"

Jesus, that is a question I have for You. If I had my choice, I would never leave your presence. Just as Moses was on the mountaintop with You, or in the tent of meeting with You, I want to stay here with You. I know I have to go to the people. When? How? How can I keep the responsibilities of this world and stay here with You?

I see Him smile and look ever so tenderly at me. "One step at a time." Jesus offers His hand and brings me to His side. I look down at my feet and see His next to mine on the beautiful golden path.

Dialogue 23

True Value Before Us

"He gave some to be apostles; and some, prophets; and some, evangelists; and some, shepherds and teachers; for the perfecting of the saints, to the work of serving, to the building up of the body of Christ; until we all attain to the unity of the faith, and of the knowledge of the Son of God, to a full grown man, to the measure of the stature of the fullness of Christ; that we may no longer be children, tossed back and forth and carried about with every wind of doctrine, by the trickery of men, in craftiness, after the wiles of error; but speaking truth in love, we may grow up in all things into him, who is the head, Christ; from whom all the body, being fitted and knit together through that which every joint supplies, according to the working in measure of each individual part, makes the body increase to the building up of itself in love." - Ephesians 4:11-16 (WEB)

The Anticipation

"...but speaking truth in love, we may grow up in all things into him, who is the head, Christ" - Ephesians 4:15 (WEB)

What do you value? Why do you value it? What makes something have great worth to you?

What do you think the Scripture means when it says, "Till we all come to the unity of the faith and the knowledge of the Son of God?" Do you think that's achievable? Why or why not?

What do you think God values? (See Matthew 25:34-46; Luke 19:10; John 13:34, 35; and I John 3:23 for the answers.)

The Conversation

We are standing on top of a large mountain with a magnificent view before us. The skies are blue, the sun warm, and the air crisp.

"Drink in the sight."

I stand there marveling at all the glory of God's creation before me. The magnitude makes me feel so small in comparison. Green trees cover the ridges like blankets as far as I can see. Everything looks fresh, strong and healthy so that I cannot see into the valleys.

"Do you understand the value of these mountains?"

Value? I guess I never before considered mountains having a 'value'. Well, I guess that depends on who you are talking to. Each person, from his own perspective, would have a different value. Some may say they can be bought, others say they couldn't. How, Lord, would You answer Your question?

He scans the landscape and points to a certain spot on the mountain side across from us. I focus on where He is pointing. Somehow Jesus brings that area into closer view. As He does, I see a clearing through the trees. Nestled inside is an average wood home with a family and kids outside. They are working, each diligent in their own tasks. They appear to be a family who is close and love each other. Their faces light up with smiles as they laugh and chat while they work. Then Jesus draws us back to the original spot we were standing on the mountain. The family is now hidden from my view.

He looks at me then turns towards the mountains. "What is the value of those mountains?"

I now understand. The mountains are not just land, trees, acres, resources and tourist spots. Those mountains are people. They are priceless, Lord.

"Priceless." He says softly. "Truly priceless."

He sits me down in front of Him. "The world does not see as I see. Even Christians have disagreements and conflicts over things that do not really matter. They still see with their eyes. Stewardship, value, accountability, treasure, these are all words people translate into worldly things, including Christians. No, they are so much more. So much more priceless and the accountability will be much greater. Children, spouse, My truth, people, the lost, the saved…" I see Him put His hands to His chest and bring forth something most beautiful. Light radiates from his strong hands. "Love. That is the true definitions for these words. They have eternal value and shall be required by everyone as an accounting for these things."

"Many put programs and money and property into the equation when it should never be there. Did I have a building to preach and teach? Did I have programs and marketing techniques to persuade the masses? No. I gave love and truth and the power of God into the lives of those who desired to know My Father. All those other things can be used, but they are not to be weighted like they are. I can tear down, and I will! I can build up, and I will!"

My heart sinks and rejoices at the same time. It sinks because I know how we have been taught in the church. I can hear even now the responses from people to what He just said. There will be some who will argue that no church can reach the people without a building and the church has to pay its bills, etc. In contrast, we need to understand how this is not to be given the same standing as, or in the place of love. At the same time I rejoice because of the freedom and the truth of His words! Love is the greatest treasure, the greatest value, the greatest power we can know. And through His love we can raise our children, love our spouses, disciple our brethren, save the lost. I understand in a new way how and why we will be accountable for these things. The standard of the measure will be love.

Jesus gazes at the mountains again. "All this shall pass away." The mountains fade before us as His pure light floods around us. People are walking as if stepping out of the mountains into the light towards Jesus. Their faces are lit with great joy as Jesus welcomes them warmly. "But My words and My love shall never pass away."

Dialogue 24

Creating My Future

"Don't lay up treasures for yourselves on the earth, where moth and rust consume, and where thieves break through and steal; but lay up for yourselves treasures in heaven, where neither moth nor rust consume, and where thieves don't break through and steal; for where your treasure is, there your heart will be also. - Matthew 6:19-21 (WEB)

The Anticipation

For where your treasure is, there your heart will be also. - Matthew 6:21 (WEB)

Have you given much thought to what you treasure in this life? List some of the things, people, items, or institutions that you value greatly.

How can these items influence your life, your sense of happiness, joy or self-satisfaction?

Consider some of your personal pursuits and goals in light of the following verses: Matthew 6:22 and 33; Matthew 13:44, 52; Luke 6:45; Luke 12:21; II Corinthians 4:7

The Conversation

As we sit in the meadow with all of perfection surrounding me, Jesus says, "You can tie branches together with the cord of unity."

I do not understand, Lord.

"Many call upon My name for their desires to be achieved. From My perspective and the view I have over their lives, much must be bound up for either the fire or for the storehouse. The heart stores the treasures of one's life, to be hidden from view of others. I alone can see. Not only do I see what is stored, but also why. I can also see how the treasure is attached to either a truth or a lie. These treasures create the desires that burn within a person. The flesh and the spirit of a man tend to follow after these desires."

"Salvation frees the heart from the claim of the world in relation to a man's heart. At that point My truth enters into the heart and brings light inside revealing the desires as well as their roots. This is why I command My followers to disciple and teach all I have commanded. My word and My truth will root out any lies, sin, and hidden evil within the life of a man, including his heart. Salvation is only the beginning of one's eternal life. From salvation, the regeneration of one's new life begins. These fledgling souls, My little children, need a balance of love and discipline, fertilizer and weeding so to speak, in order to grow strong in their faith."

"Remember the song, 'Abiding in Jesus'?"

I do not recall the song so I get up to look for it. The song is by Barney Warren and I read through it quickly. (See the lyrics at the end of this chapter.) I do not see any connection to what He is teaching me.

"Read the lyrics, slowly, carefully. Look at the change that has taken place within the writer as he proclaims what I have done. Can you imagine what is in his heart or on his mind? What are the desires within him?"

I read through the song again, slowly this time. I am looking for what Jesus mentioned specifically. I begin to see from Barney Warren's words a man who was declaring that he is now free. He sees his life as blessed now, being cared for by Jesus and enjoying His love. He is cheerful, happy and enjoying pleasures that are rich compared to what he had before in the world. He considers it sweet his victory over the tempter. He also declares the bliss he knows because he now has eternal life. He is abiding in You every moment and every hour which fills him with joy inexpressible. He is proclaiming that You are more and far better than anything this world has to offer.

"One's focus determines what rules in one's heart, which in turn determines the course of action one takes as he goes through the day. From one moment to the next, one step to the next, your focus will determine what happens – in the near future and in the far."

I begin to understand what He is saying. Not only do the decisions we make now determine our future actions, but they indicate the desires of our heart. Truly the goals we have set before us determine the decisions we make now - they are intertwined. No wonder we so easily get caught in a trap! We do create our own world, our own struggles and conflicts. It is as if when I wake up in the morning and know what I have to get done with work and family, I make 'Work' and 'Family' my goal and priority. These things are not bad or wrong, but every action, every thought I have is focused on achieving that goal. So, as the day passes and things do not go as I planned, then I get frustrated, angry, or overwhelmed. This happens even on days I have started with God or tried to seek Him throughout the day. On the other hand, if I had put 'Growing Closer to God' as my priority and goal for the day, then whatever does or does not get done on my list is all in God's care, not mine. I have noticed the days that I have focused on God in such a way, I got more accomplished with more peace, even when things did go wrong.

What a subtle difference! I understand, Lord! I see it is all through Scripture, from Genesis to Revelation: Focus on God, love God with all our heart, mind, soul and strength, fight the good fight, run the race, obey, be holy, meditate on Your Word, and the list goes on. Every decision we make affects the next step all the way through to the future far ahead. Eternal life starts at salvation, but our spiritual life, the quality of that life, is determined by what our heart treasures and in the knowing that we have an eternal home waiting on us. I read again the song. Barney Warren found great joy, "bliss" he said, knowing every moment he was experiencing God's eternal life.

"As you stand and walk in the course I have prepared for you, your faith shall become a beacon to others as a testimony beyond any of your imaginations. This is My fruit in your life and it is far more valuable than anything this world has to offer."

Lord, may I experience such extreme joy and peace every moment of every day as Barney Warren described. Help me, remind me to make You my goal and my priority as I wake every morning and as I walk through the day. May You and You alone be my heart's desire!

Abiding in Jesus

Barney E. Warren, pub.1911
Copyright: Public Domain

1. I'm abiding in Jesus, what a blessed place!
I am sure He kindly cares for me;
He will never forsake me if I trust His grace,
In His cleansing blood, I now am free.

Refrain:
I'm abiding in the Savior's love,
He kindly cares for me;
I'm abiding in the Savior's love;
In Him my soul is free.

2. I'm abiding in Jesus, what a cheering thought!
Earthly joys grow dim and pass away;
I am happy in knowing that His grace has brought
Pleasures rich that never will decay.

3. I'm abiding in Jesus everywhere I go,
In His sweet embrace, I'm safe from harm;
Of His spirit in fullness we may surely know,
I am leaning on the Savior's arm.

4. I'm abiding in Jesus, oh, His rest is sweet!
And His grace will foil the tempter's power;
Life eternal with gladness in my soul complete,
Is a source of bliss to me each hour.

Dialogue 25

My Truth Never Changes

"But they worship me in vain, teaching as doctrines the commandments of men. For you set aside the commandment of God, and hold tightly to the tradition of men—the washing of pitchers and cups, and you do many other such things." He said to them, "Full well do you reject the commandment of God, that you may keep your tradition." - Mark 7:7-9 (WEB)

The Anticipation

"For you set aside the commandment of God, and hold tightly to the tradition of men..." - Mark 7:8(a) (WEB)

What are some of the traditions, beliefs and habits that you see people cling to that seem to be contradictory to the Scripture? Why do you think it is difficult for people to embrace the truth?

Do you think it is possible that you might have been taught certain things about the Bible and God that are not true? If yes, how does that knowledge make you feel? What steps can you take to either confirm or challenge some of the teachings you cling too?

Read II Timothy 3:16 and 17. The Bible assures us that God's truth is found in the Scriptures. Today ask yourself, "Am I clinging to what man has taught me and ignoring Scriptures that contradict my views?" Pray and ask Jesus to begin to change your heart and mind so you can receive His truth. Pray that the Holy Spirit will teach you His ultimate truth. (See also John 14:26; 15:26)

The Conversation

"This is all the truth that can reside within one who follows Me – only that which the person can embrace and receive."

I do not understand.

"Although I am truth, not only by title but also in essence, man has limitations because of his beliefs. Faith opens an understanding of truth within a person that exemplifies a portion of the truth that his faith has received, not with fear, but in love. Remember Hebrews 11:1 where it is written *Faith is the substance of things hoped for, the evidence of things not seen*? Faith not only drives the thoughts and actions of a person, but also allows or brings situations into his life like one who writes on a chalkboard or paper."

"Just as you have a belief that the workings of drinking or doing drugs are dangerous not only for you, but your family, you act accordingly. You protect yourself and your family by staying clear of situations, not only physically, but also from the music, the movies, the literature, and other influences that could possibly come to you and be contrary to this truth that you know. When you do so, you are also removing the writing of harmful situations into your life. This allows Me to be able to teach you more of My truth as well as use you to help in other lives to bring them closer to Me."

Jesus pauses and then asks, "Can people have faith in things, ideas or teachings that are not truth?"

Yes, Lord, I believe so.

"Correct. Faith is what? The substance one believes is true. It is also the cause and result of the evidence of what is within a person's heart and mind. That is why, when you look through eyes of truth and love, you are able to inspect the fruit of a person's life and know what one believes. People try so hard to hide, to cover, to justify, to protect their form of truth which is their faith, that they can completely miss the workings of My Word and My Spirit in not only their lives, but also in the lives of those around them. Truth to them is what they want. You have struggled with some of My truth because it was not what you wanted. Your focus was on a specific application or understanding, even a desire that you wanted to make fit. But the issue was that the truth is then lost when it is conformed to fit into the understanding or usage of a person. Instead, the person needs to conform and change through My Spirit in order to receive the fullness of My truth."

"My truth never changes; it is the same from the beginning to the end. Man cannot adjust or twist or even redefine My truth, although he tries to convince himself and others of such a rebellious act. No, rather, man must be the one to be changed by My truth so one can enter into not only an intimate relationship with Me, but also with others. Oh, how the depth of deceptions has grown by just this one understanding of how man perceives the truth as he wants it! A person even sees the inconsistencies or non-logic of the beliefs, but he wants his desires so intensely, he is willing to surrender himself, and his faith, to the lie."

Dialogue 26

Truth and Perception

"But when day had already come, Jesus stood on the beach, yet the disciples didn't know that it was Jesus. Jesus therefore said to them, 'Children, have you anything to eat?'

They answered him, 'No.'

He said to them, 'Cast the net on the right side of the boat, and you will find some.'

They cast it therefore, and now they weren't able to draw it in for the multitude of fish. That disciple therefore whom Jesus loved said to Peter, 'It's the Lord!'

So when Simon Peter heard that it was the Lord, he wrapped his coat around him (for he was naked), and threw himself into the sea." - John 21:4-7 (WEB)

The Anticipation

"So when Simon Peter heard that it was the Lord, he wrapped his coat around him (for he was naked), and threw himself into the sea." - John 21:7 (WEB)

Consider the various relationships Jesus had while He was on the earth. Many saw Him from a distance while others knew Him more intimately. The disciples had a very close relationship with Jesus. They ate with Him, walked with Him, slept near Him. Some disciples seemed even closer to Jesus than others. John was described as the one who loved the Lord and who was loved by Him, while Peter was known to demonstrate extravagant expressions of devotion.

Think about your closest relationship. Whether it be a family member or a friend, what are the elements that make this relationship close? How would you compare your relationship with Jesus to that relationship? Are you as close to Jesus as you are in that relationship? Why or why not?

What kind of a relationship do you want with Jesus? And what are you willing to do to achieve it?

The Conversation

The Lord shows me a man standing before a pastor of a church. I am granted the view from the eyes of the man and his perception of the pastor. He sees the position of the pastor with a shallow understanding of the man himself. Their relationship is at a professional level and no more. Although the pastor knows much about the personal life of the man, the parishioner does not know, nor cares to know, who the pastor is as an individual.

The scene changes to the pastor interacting with his family. I now see him through his family's eyes as he interacts with them freely. The family has an intimate relationship with him and loves him very much. They know the pastor's views and feelings, failures and fears, yet love him with a deep and forgiving love. This love is a mutual love, given and taken within the family.

Then I see the Lord standing before me. "How do you see Me?"

Somewhere in between the two scenarios, Lord. I see You as God, all powerful with authority. Yet, I am learning more about You personally through the Bible and our relationship.

"What relationship do you desire to have with Me?"

I think about it a moment. I desire a deep, intimate relationship with You based on trust and truth in all areas. I also want a relationship with You that is reciprocated. Not one-sided, but given and received both ways.

"Yes, child. A relationship is based on the expectations, perceptions, and dynamics of each person involved. Look at the accounts with Me and My disciples as well as the other followers. Some people who followed Me wanted only what they could receive from Me. Notice how when the teachings became too hard for them or when I requested something of them, they left Me. They had a relationship with Me based only upon the truth of Me that they wanted to embrace. It was nowhere near a complete or encompassing view of My truth, but only the part they wanted. Then they added their own truth to Mine to create what they would put their faith in. Their faith then caused them to act and think the way they did. As you read through the Gospels, you notice the growth and change of My disciples, except one. He too changed, but Judas only grew deeper in what sliver of My truth He wanted. Then he added to it his own ambitions and passions for his own ideologies. Judas, along with many of the Jewish leaders, knew the Scriptures, but did not understand (nor desire to know) My truth in the Scriptures. They read and taught them to fit their own selfish desires. They have received the fullness of their rewards."

Jesus changes the view around us in an instant. We are walking along a beach and I realize we are at the Sea of Galilee. As the waves gently lap the shore I focus in on Jesus' words.

"Now notice the rest of the disciples. Even when I walked on the earth, I met each one where he was. Did you know that each one was prepared to become my disciple? They were created to be Mine. Each was different, which meant he had a unique relationship with Me. I loved them, taught them, challenged them and ministered to them as each needed Me to. Many would actually say I did not treat them fairly, for John, Peter and James were My closest. These three, though, desired a deeper relationship with Me. They desired more truth, more understanding of Father and My Kingdom. I will not withhold from those who hunger and thirst for My truth. In contrast, I will withhold My truth from those who distort it and use it for their selfish gain or for deceit. They will become as dry bones in the desert sands. They may be rich, but one day, everything will be required from them. They will stand before Me and give an account for what they have done."

"Just as the pastor had many different relationships, so do I. Each person's relationship to Me is unique. I am different from the pastor though. Every person who comes to Me through faith is a child of God. I am not a respecter of persons in the sense of favoritism as the world defines it. I do have different purposes and plans for each person. Not only do I respect each person, but also his desire of a relationship with Me. Some will come to Me only with the understanding of My position and have trouble seeing me as their friend. Others may want Me as friend, but will not want to surrender to Me their lives, in part or in whole, as Lord. You see, I can only go as far into a relationship with someone to the extent he is desiring with Me. All of this is based on his understanding and acceptance of My truth."

Lord, why is it difficult to grasp and accept Your truth? Your truth is so simple and perfect, yet we seem to make it hard. It seems like most people think that Your truth is only a set of suggestions that they can choose from. I know that this should not be the way we respond to your truth.

Jesus stoops down and picks up a shell. He holds the shell out to me. It is a complete shell, dark with lines on it. It looks kind of like a snail shell.

"What is the truth about this shell?"

Well, I do not know from where it came or what animal lived in it. I can presume quite a bit since it was sitting here by the water, but honestly, I would only be presuming.

"Yes, you are right, you would be presuming." He continues to hold it as we start to walk on the beach. "Everything you see, is processed within you with your own intellect, imaginations, beliefs," He looks at me, "and your own desires. If you want to think this shell came from an animal that lived in this sea, you could. Maybe, you wanted to think it came from a child who was playing with a collection he had brought from home. On the other hand, you may have wanted to think this came from a trader from a far away land. So again, I ask, what is the truth concerning this shell?"

Only You, since You are God, and any eyewitnesses of the history of this specific shell would be able to tell the truth about it.

"What can the eyewitnesses say about it?"

Only what they have seen regarding it and what others may have said about it. Yet, other people's words would still be filtered through their own understanding.

"Exactly. Perception and truth are two different things. Now, if I spoke the truth about this shell to those around us on the beach, they would most likely mock us for it would not fit into their belief system. If they do that with a simple shell that has such little value or impact on their lives, what do you think they will do with My truth?"

They will have a tendency to dismiss or reject it because it conflicts with what they have believed for so many years.

I understand, Lord.

Dialogue 27

Words of Life

"In the fourth watch of the night, Jesus came to them, walking on the sea. When the disciples saw him walking on the sea, they were troubled, saying, "It's a ghost!" and they cried out for fear. But immediately Jesus spoke to them, saying "Cheer up! It is I! Don't be afraid."

Peter answered him and said, "Lord, if it is you, command me to come to you on the waters."

He said, "Come!"

Peter stepped down from the boat, and walked on the waters to come to Jesus. But when he saw that the wind was strong, he was afraid, and beginning to sink, he cried out, saying, "Lord, save me!" - Matthew 14:25-30 (WEB)

The Anticipation

"But immediately Jesus spoke to them, saying 'Cheer up! It is I! Don't be afraid.'" - *Matthew 14:27 (WEB)*

"Be of good cheer! It is I; do not be afraid." How these words can be music to our ears, especially when we are frightened. Many of us have probably experienced a time when we were startled only to discover a familiar voice reassure us not to be afraid. With the realization we are near someone safe our fear quickly turns into relief and even joy. To hear Jesus declare, "Don't be afraid, it is I," must have been so comforting in the midst of the storm.

Peter filled with faith at these words asks Jesus to let him come, and defying the laws of gravity and any sense of reason this experienced fisherman steps out of the boat and onto the water. I wonder what thoughts could have gone through his head in those first few moments.

Was he astounded, thrilled, excited? How soon did his thoughts shift to the storm raging around him? How long did he take before he began to wonder how this was possible, perhaps even contemplate that impossibility of what he was doing? We may never know, but what we do know is that he took his focus off of Jesus and that caused him to doubt.

Read the story in its entirety. Start with verse 22 and go to verse 36. Note the sequence of events and how the disciples end up declaring that Jesus is the Son of God. How can you apply this event to your life? How can keeping your focus on Jesus help you personally?

The Conversation

He asks if I want to hear a story.

I smile. Yes! A story from the Creator Himself, definitely!

He brings me back to the Sea of Galilee. I stand amazed at its vastness and beauty. I look down at the sand. It is not soft white Florida sand, nor is it that hard dirty soil. This area is somewhat in-between: rough, speckled dark and light. The sea seems so large, Lord.

He smiles, "Yes, it is large."

We sit down on the sand.

"Over there, " He points to the distance to the right, "Was where I walked on the water in the storm to My disciples."

"When Peter walked on water?" I asked.

"Yes. He did." I see the dark waves rolling, the Lord walking toward the boat, the fear on the men's faces as they fight the waves while trying to comprehend His appearance. I hear them cry out to Him and His response. Then Peter asks the Lord if he can come to Him. Suddenly, I am overwhelmed as I sense what Peter felt at that moment. I feel his joy, mingled with faith, love and an anticipation of what may happen soon. He is so drawn to Jesus that nothing is between him and the Lord. Jesus gives

His command to Peter to come. Peter, with his eyes fixed intently upon Jesus, gets out of the boat and walks on the water to his Lord.

I realize something immediately that never clicked with me before. You did not stop the waves, the wind or the storm before he got out of the boat. You could have, but You didn't! I now have a deeper understanding of how God works. Jesus doesn't do just what needs to be done for a moment. He designs or choreographs every element of a situation in such a way so that His perfect plan, lesson, or will gets accomplished to the fullest extent.

Jesus nods.

Then Peter notices the waves all of the sudden like they had been absent up until now. He begins to sink. Even then Jesus does not stop the storm. Jesus waits patiently until Peter calls to Him. Jesus reaches down and raises Peter to him in the midst of the waves and wind. Then they both walk together to the boat and climb in.

"My child, faith, joy, love and peace fill those who are so focused on Me, they do not even notice the storm around them." Then He looks at me. "You must do the same. You cannot heed the lies and words of the world, the people or even worry about how you are perceived by others. You must focus on Me. Focus on Me with all your heart, all your soul, all your mind, and all your strength! Then no matter what the world, the enemy or people throw at you, it will have no effect. Know that you will fall, stumble, say the wrong thing, or do something incorrect. Do you realize that Peter could have taken a misstep, said the wrong word or tripped, yet he would not have sunk as long as his focus was on Me? Walk with confidence in who I am. Then I will hold you up."

Dialogue 28

A Glimpse of Heaven

"I saw a new heaven and a new earth: for the first heaven and the first earth have passed away, and the sea is no more. I saw the holy city, New Jerusalem, coming down out of heaven from God, prepared like a bride adorned for her husband. I heard a loud voice out of heaven saying, 'Behold, God's dwelling is with people, and he will dwell with them, and they will be his people, and God himself will be with them as their God. He will wipe away from them every tear from their eyes. Death will be no more; neither will there be mourning, nor crying, nor pain, any more. The first things have passed away.'" - Revelation 21:1-4 (WEB)

The Anticipation

"...Death will be no more; neither will there be mourning, nor crying, nor pain, any more. The first things have passed away." - Revelation 21: 4(b) (WEB)

The Apostle John writes about His glimpse into the New Heaven and New Earth. In the above verses he describes a place where the people of God will dwell for all of eternity. A place without tears, without sorrow, without death.

Philippians 3:14 talks about pursuing a prize, one obviously worth striving for. Verse 13 in the same passage encourages us to forget what is behind us and reach out for those things that still lie ahead. As followers of Jesus we need to remember that all of eternity with all of its rewards and blessings lies before us. In fact many of our elderly need to remember that they aren't ending a stage of life as much as they are in the beginning phases of transition. Those of us who are advanced in years need to take this time to prepare our hearts. At the same time, those of us who are younger need to remember that we are in a race that must be completed. That race begins when we accept Jesus as our Lord and Savior, but it doesn't end until we reach eternity's gates.

No matter what stage of life you are in you can do your part to share with others about the amazing prize that awaits. Heaven is not only our goal, it is our home. Our job is to bring as many people with us as we possibly can, and that can only be accomplished when we tell others about Jesus. It seems too often life's struggles, disappointments and riches can get us off course. What are some things in your life that you are still clinging to? Are any of those items interfering with your race towards the prize? Ask Jesus to help you to overcome so that you can stay the course.

The Conversation

It has been a long, tough day. So many issues and demands presented themselves to me today that I made several mistakes. Even through my frustration and anger with myself, things seemed to turn out all right. I am still discouraged for making such simple errors. As I pray, the Lord draws near to me.

Jesus looks intently into my eyes, "Love. Love, My child. Love covers a multitude of sins. Even though others may see your mistakes, I cover your mistakes in love when you are walking with Me. Walk humbly before Me, in faith focusing on Me, and I will empower you to do miraculous things."

I process what He had just said, focusing on the words He had just spoken.

"You are Mine, you are loved dearly."

I smile as I look at Him. All eternity, Lord? I ask with a hopeful heart pounding with expectancy as a child would.

His smile warms my heart, "All eternity. All eternity."

He looks up and I follow His gaze. A sea appears before us. Suddenly, the view before me splits in two and the sides pull away from each other like curtains. Behind the fading view of the ocean is the brightest, shiniest, purest, most beautiful place I had ever seen. He smiles as I stand up staring at what I know in my heart is eternity - beyond anything and everything I know.

Scenes flash in front of me of things I cannot describe. All I can comprehend with my mind is the limitless vastness of all eternity in dimensions I cannot fathom. It is like every thought I had before of what Heaven would be like was as a speck of dust in comparison to the truth before me. I start to walk toward eternity. My heart is intensely drawn to it filled with longing and desire. Jesus gently takes my hand.

"No, child, you can't go now."

I stop and turn to Jesus. But, Lord, I want to go now.

"Not now. You will be here soon enough. You need to bring as many as you can with you."

I relax and trust His instructions. Within me rises a just as strong desire to continue working for Him here while I still can. He is worthy of every moment, every ounce of strength I can muster for Him until I enter eternity to rest.

Oh, how can I share Your truth so others will understand? I need You, Lord, I need You! I need You to show me and teach me how to expound upon your Scriptures so as to teach others about You. Help me to share that everyone needs You.

Dialogue 29

Children in His Eyes

"They were bringing to him little children, that he should touch them, but the disciples rebuked those who were bringing them. But when Jesus saw it, he was moved with indignation, and said to them, 'Allow the little children to come to me! Don't forbid them, for God's Kingdom belongs to such as these. Most certainly I tell you, whoever will not receive God's Kingdom like a little child, he will in no way enter into it.' He took them in his arms, and blessed them, laying his hands on them." - Mark 10:13-16 (WEB)

The Anticipation

"He took them in his arms, and blessed them, laying his hands on them." - Mark 10:16 (WEB)

Jesus treasures children and desires to bless them. Since He values them so much, in what areas are you willing to let Him help you love and bless the children in your life?

Why do you think Jesus tells us we can only come to Him if we come as a child? What do you think it means to enter His Kingdom as a child?

Reflect a moment on this question; try to seek God for the answer. Are you supposed to have the faith of a child only for salvation or does Jesus desire you to continue in that childlike faith in your Christian walk?

The Conversation

"Children have the capacity to give and receive love in purity and truth, especially when they have not been hurt by another. I was serious about My warning to those who hurt My little ones. My little ones are children, and those of a pure faith, filled with innocence and hope, joy and trust in Me. They reflect My love and glory with the least added contamination. Come with Me."

I follow the Lord. He holds my hand as we walk on the amazing gold path that grows with each of His steps. He takes me to a busy intersection of an inner city neighborhood.

Lord, I want to see more clearly. Not my imagination, but only Your revelation. I look to Jesus and then I look around. We have stopped in an alley. Not just any back alley area but one that includes the intersection of other alleys like very small streets. I see about twenty people who are walking around, standing, or watching others. Most are wearing dirty old clothes with disheveled hair. The area is lit only by the light from the sun in the sky as it peeks through the tall buildings surrounding us. I see clearly here only because the glory from Jesus is lighting up the area around us. The air is warm, almost stifling with the lack of air flow. There are brick and concrete buildings surrounding us with pallets, garbage and old boxes haphazardly stacked through the alley ways. I am amazed by the noise and yet few are talking.

Lord, I sense confusion here and a busyness I cannot explain or even see. What I sense and see are two different things.

"First, tell Me what you see the people doing. Do not be afraid."

I see three men standing up against the wall. They mumble with each other in very low voices as they watch the people around them. There is a young teen girl, eyes down, walking quickly through, trying not to be noticed. An older man is sitting in the corner, not really coherent or acknowledging what is going on around him. Other small groups are just walking by acting oblivious to those around, yet I know they are keenly aware of every detail. A woman with a young girl is quickly and quietly trying to get past.

"Now, see with My eyes."

I close my eyes for a moment, trying to take the courage to open my eyes in expectation of seeing through them as my Lord would. Lord, remove any preconceived ideas and my own imaginations. I want only Your truth.

I open my eyes to see the area brightly lit up. There are no shadows, no darkness, nothing is hidden. The wall, garbage, pallets, everything of the world seem almost transparent. As we walk toward the man sitting in the corner, I can almost see through him. He appears empty with an extreme burden or weight around him. The sense of emptiness is overwhelming as we walk closer to him. Then I see them. There are a handful of small dark spirits beneath him and behind him. They appear to be trying to hide from Jesus. Yet, at the same time, they are trying to muster up courage because of their legal right to be with the man. There are thick chains in the man's hands. Because of his grip on the chains, it is almost like the dark spirits were tied to him and the chains were tied to the spirits.

Can he let go, Lord? Or do they have him chained?

"Yes, both. He can let go if He wants to open his hand and grab for Mine. Yet in a way, they have his hand grasping their chain. It is tied to him, yet ultimately it is his choice to let go. He can't though, until he has hope. That hope is only found in Me and My Word."

Does he know You? A movie about a boy begins to play before us. I understand it is a memory from the man's past.

"He heard My truth in a church Vacation Bible School program when he was ten. What he heard conflicted with what he saw at home. His abuse was great. His pain was deep. He wanted to believe, but dismissed it all as fairy tales. He has met other Christians, but could not let go of the lies and the pain to grasp for even the smallest amount of hope. He has a choice too. I cannot come and break down the strongholds without his request. If I did, it would not be love that saves. Grace, mercy, compassion and love, they all have to be received, not pushed upon or forced onto."

Then He shows me the three men by the wall. Lord, one is faintly lit.

"Yes, he is one who will choose Me soon. The seed has been planted by his grandmother. She still prays for him. I am waiting for a moment in his life when I will be able to speak to him. Several have watered him with My truth. His anger and unforgiveness keeps him justifying to himself that his way is best. You see how he is a bit separated from the others; he does not fully accept their words. He is with them and yet in a way, he is not. He is conflicted inside and does not know why."

I see warfare around him. The dark ones are near him and there is also a tall bright angel by him.

"The angel is sent by My Father. He knows when to fight and when to wait. He knows just how much to protect the boy and how much to release. My Spirit guides not only the angel, but the boy and even circumstances around him. All are working in perfect unity to bring the boy to a point of repentance. Most times, what is needed is a great pain, a loss, a sorrow to the soul. I do not desire to bring such pain into the lives of people, but many do not respond to repentance any other way. You see the spark, the faint light from within him? That is because he desires to know the truth. He does, deep inside, call to God although he does not know what god or who. He is seeking truth. He knows all around him is emptiness and hopelessness. Yet, he knows inside there is a hope to be found somewhere. Remember, I have written My law, My name, and My truth upon all the hearts of men. Many rebel against that truth. They rebel fully with every fiber of their being, rejecting Me and rejecting My truth. There are many others trapped by the circumstances of the world. Many who want to believe are hurt, lied to or cast aside. You were one of them. Your pain, your loss, your suffering was great, so you reached for pleasure and anything you could to release you of that pain. Yet, you knew I existed. You knew I was here even though you did not know who I was, or how I could exist."

All at once I remembered my favorite bible story. I had come across it once in Grandma's Bible. It was a story about King Solomon who was sitting in judgment over two women who had two babies. One baby died and so the mother of the dead baby took the other woman's baby as her own. The dispute was brought before the king and his wisdom brought forth the truth and saved the life of the baby. I always marveled at this story. Why Lord, did that one speak to me so?

"You have desired truth your whole life, although many times you struggled against it. King Solomon was gentle in finding the truth of a situation. Just a few words brought forth the truth in the women. Then his respect for the truth, the life of the baby and the real mother was shown as he gave the baby back to his mother. Yes My child, you have desired the truth and sought after it, even when you were confused."

Then the Lord reminds me of the Lutheran Church I went to when I was sixteen. I had asked the minister questions about God, the Bible and the Flood. He was so patient with me. I also remember the questions about God I used to ask my manager at work as a teenager. Then He shows me the books I had read. I remember even the ones that went against God's truth that I read because I was diligently seeking.

"That is why, when you had the heartbreak you did, I was there. It was a point where I could come in and reveal to you My great love for you. And you received it. Once you tasted of My glory and My love, you wanted to know what happened and the truth. You had tasted what you had always been looking for and this allowed your classmate to share with you the truth of My love."

"This man will be the same. He is seeking, looking for truth, whatever it is. I will answer him when he is ready to receive My love and truth. How can I reveal something to a person that he is not even looking for? If a man is not wanting it or desiring it, he will totally miss it. A man has the will to desire truth or deny truth. When I do reveal Myself to him, he still has the option to choose Me or deny Me. Any other way would not be love. My love is a gentle love, a respectful love, and at the same time, the most powerful love that can and will destroy all that is against Me. When one desires to not be with Me, My love which is based on truth, will honor that request. Love cannot do or be otherwise." (Hebrews 11:6)

I begin to understand new depths of truth found within II Corinthians 6:2, *"For He says, in the time of My favor I heard you and in the day of salvation I helped you."* Yes, Lord, your mercy and love are beyond our understanding, and yet, you are everything I want.

Dialogue 30

Meaning of Life

"God said, 'Let us make man in our image, after our likeness: and let them have dominion over the fish of the sea, and over the birds of the sky, and over the livestock, and over all the earth, and over every creeping thing that creeps on the earth.' God created man in his own image. In God's image he created him; male and female he created them.'" - Genesis 1:26, 27 (WEB)

The Anticipation

"God said, 'Let us make man in our image, after our likeness…'" - Genesis 1:26(a) (WEB)

Take a moment to read Genesis 1 and Genesis 2:4-7. It is the history of the heavens and the earth; the account of creation. Notice how God created all things, He simply spoke them into being. How did He create man? And who is man supposed to resemble?

In Genesis 2:8, we see that God planted the Garden of Eden Himself. Notice the care and delight He has taken in creating His universe and man. What needs to take place in order for you to have a successful garden? What kind of planning, tending and work need to happen? How are you like the garden in God's eyes?

Read Acts 17:26-31. We see that God's attention to detail doesn't stop with Genesis. According to this passage each of us has been appointed a time so we can seek the Lord Jesus. Why? The answer is found in Revelation 21:3-7

The Conversation

"You are the design of My hand and My thoughts. My design is not complete until you are with Me in eternity. I am shaping you and forming you still to be made into the image of Myself for My glory."

Lord, I submit myself to You, please do not stop working in my life. I realize I have stubborn areas and areas in which I lack self-control. Please be patient and help me grow to be what You desire me to be.

"As a master gardener tills, cultivates, and prepares the ground, so do I. Also, as he plants, trains, prunes and fertilizes a plant, so do I. Much of what a gardener does as he tends the garden, I also do with My children. There are times of watering and fertilizing so the heart of My child can grow and mature in My grace and joy. There are also times of hardening. These are times of, as a plant would experience, wind, drought and disease. These trials and tribulations help to strengthen My children so they can learn to endure with joy as they continue to focus on Me."

"One's strength is matched only by the resolve and trust one has in Me. See the man who has power and authority over others due to his position and wealth? Do you also see how he is powerless against the powers and principalities of realms beyond this world? All the powers that can be mustered up in those realms are nothing in comparison to Me. A person will get sick, lose relationships and even die because all of truth has been removed from his life, thereby removing any hope or joy that could have filled him to overflowing. The measure of a person is not in things you can see, but only in the indwelling of My Spirit within a man."

"Of all the children ever born, who would be the greatest?"

Only You, Jesus. All the rest of us are merely human. The only thing that gives us any significance is You abiding in us.

"Yes, many who have surrendered all, will be not only greater, but experience a greater hope, joy, and love because of the indwelling of Me. Nothing compares to what I have to offer. Nothing in all creation can satisfy or fulfill as I can. I have created man for My glory. That also means that I have created him to receive My glory. He is designed for My glory in receiving and reflecting from and to Me. This cannot be done on his own, for what can man give? He can give nothing of himself that has value or riches or can even sustain anything eternal in value. I have designed man to receive and contain, as well as radiate, My glory, My goodness to others and to Myself. Now miracles can happen around him. Can you see how that which is from Me affects the life of one to Me?"

Yes, in a way, Lord. I realize it will take time to understand the fullness of the truth You are speaking.

Dialogue 31

Purpose of Conflict

"We know that all things work together for good for those who love God, to those who are called according to his purpose. For whom he foreknew, he also predestined to be conformed to the image of his Son, that he might be the firstborn among many brothers. Whom he predestined, those he also called. Whom he called, those he also justified. Whom he justified, those he also glorified. What then shall we say about these things? If God is for us, who can be against us? He who didn't spare his own Son, but delivered him up for us all, how would he not also with him freely give us all things?" - Romans 8:28-32 (WEB)

The Anticipation

"We know that all things work together for good for those who love God, to those who are called according to his purpose." - Romans 8:28 (WEB)

None of us likes adversity. We strive to avoid it at all cost, yet the Bible says that God works all things together for our good, even bad things. We tend to miss the benefits that can come with conflict and fail to realize how our struggles can benefit us. Often adversity draws us closer to God, makes us stronger or even causes us to change an unhealthy lifestyle. Can you think of a time when a personal conflict, trial or time of adversity benefited your spiritual development? What was the conflict and what good things did happen as a result?

Examine Proverbs 27:6, 17. In what ways do these two Proverbs apply to your life and your relationships? Do you realize how difficult people in your life sharpen you?

The Conversation

I see myself standing on a sea with the waves crashing on my feet trying to pull me in. I keep my eyes on Jesus ahead of me. I feel such joy rise within me because He is so close and empowering me to do that which I could not without Him. He smiles while encouraging me. All of a sudden I realize something incredible. I realize that there are no limitations. It is like the whole sea has glass at the surface on which the waves roll on top. As long as I trust Jesus and keep my focus on Him, I can walk, skip, run toward and around Him. There is no pride in the fact I can walk on the water. Instead, all my focus and hope is upon Jesus and I know that He alone gives me the ability to do anything.

I feel the waves roll over my feet. Then suddenly they reach up to my ankles and continue to rise up to my knees and then my hips. I feel the waves trying to pull me down into the sea. I am able to sense what those waves are and begin to identify them by name! Some waves are my business' demands, others are specific responsibilities, others waves are people I know and so on. I keep my focus on Jesus as each wave that pulls at me is revealed. I know that they are trying to pull me away from Jesus. Many are unintentionally pulling at me, but they want my attention, and they want it now!

Suddenly, everything around me for a moment is changed. I am now a part of a game or a scenario where people are trying to stop me from completing a task. Instead of focusing on the people, I focus even more intently on what I am trying to accomplish. As I continue to fight, it becomes easier to ignore the people around me. Finally, I finish the task and the people change. Now they come around me and congratulate me. Their job was to challenge and test me in order to make me stronger so I could finish the race well.

I begin to understand. We, as Christians, try to live by following Christ. Since we are human and not perfect, sometimes we hurt each other in the process. What I realize is that God is so great and so wise and wonderful, that He uses those moments to train and teach everyone involved. He may even use the experience as an opportunity to teach others who are outside of the situation.

Now I am standing before Jesus in eternity with many people around Him. The praises raised to Him from us all with joyous hearts is almost deafening. I look around the group and notice someone who had hurt me in the past. I smile as the memory flashes through my mind. The incident does not have the pain, shame and frustration it had in the past. The person sees my gaze and returns to me a sweet smile. From our view in eternity, both of us can see the past situation in a totally different light. That moment in the past happened in order to teach and train us as well as draw us both closer to Jesus. Here in eternity, there is no hurt, guilt or pain, or even resentment. We are experiencing such joy and love for God and each other that the darkness of the situation is faded completely away from view.

I hear clearly Jesus' voice, "All things work for the good of those who love Me." I smile, yes, Lord, they truly do. Thank You for Your truth. (Romans 8:28)

Dialogue 32

Judgment of Truth

"Who will give account to him who is ready to judge the living and the dead. For to this end the Good News was preached even to the dead, that they might be judged indeed as men in the flesh, but live as to God in the spirit. But the end of all things is near. Therefore be of sound mind, self-controlled, and sober in prayer. And above all things be earnest in your love among yourselves, for love covers a multitude of sins." - I Peter 4:5-8 (WEB)

The Anticipation

"Who will give account to him who is ready to judge the living and the dead." - I Peter 4:5 (WEB)

Read Revelation 22:7-16. Jesus talks about giving rewards according to our works. These rewards are a great mystery, but we know that His words are trustworthy and true. If Jesus said there would be rewards, then there will be. What are you doing to earn His rewards? (See James 1:27 to start your list.)

Revelation 20:12-15 reminds us that judgment day is coming. Where do you stand? Is your name written in the Lamb's book of life? (See John 3:16-21) Test yourself against Galatians 5:19-23. If you see you are struggling with an issue, take time to pray about it. (See I John 1:9)

The people of God sing no ordinary song in Revelation 5:7-14 but a new song. This song is composed with words of praise to the Lamb who was slain. He loved us so much He was willing to lay His life down for us. (See John 15:13) Today join in the celebration and give God thanks for what He has done for you. Those who proclaim Jesus as Lord are saved (See Romans 10:9-13), have eternal life and shall not be taken out of the Father's hand. (See Romans 8:38,39)

The Conversation

I see around me the stars of the universe as if I am standing in space. As I look around, above and below me, I see the twinkling of the shining stars like diamonds in suspension. There are clusters of brilliant colors as well as what looks like clouds stretched through large expanses. I feel neither cold nor heat, nor pressure nor lack thereof. It's like I am standing in a vacuum. I close my eyes and wait.

A song fades in as if on the wings of a breeze. No melody or words, just beautiful sound, almost like stringed instruments in harmonious unity. I feel as if I am suddenly covered with water, yet it is dry. There is a pressure, intense and yet gentle. It is comforting as it wraps around me as it begins to move and sway. I can feel the music around me and within me. The sound has become as a symphony, full and strong as the bass at a loud concert. All within me desires to proclaim, to praise God Most High! Oh for a thousand tongues to sing of Your greatness my Lord, my God! If only all who have breath would know of Your glory and power! I desire for them to know of Your majesty and love! If only all would accept the truth that You have placed within each of us that You are God and You alone are the Creator and Savior of all mankind!

"Child, this world and all that it contains, which was made by My hand, desires and groans to be made perfect again. Man has failed his charge from Me to tend and care for it as well as taking care of each other. (Genesis 1:26 and 2:15) Daily, the reminder of what man has done and is doing, continues to rise to My throne as dark, smelly smoke. My mercies and compassion on My remnant stays My hand to My side, as well as the remembrance of My promise to those who call upon My Son's name. I know the name of the last one who will cry out to Me. Then I will send My Son. He will go and bring His righteous judgment upon all that breathes and creeps upon the land or swims within the seas. There shall be none left, none who have not received the judgment of His hand. He shall bring to Me His faithful ones and remove from Our presence the rest, all who hate Me and My children. At that time, the door of all time shall be closed and everything shall be brought into perfect harmony with Us. No more sin, no more pain, no more of anything that is evil or even out of My truth. All shall be in unity with Us and with each other."

"This is truth, child. Stand on it, proclaim it! Jesus is returning for His own soon. Do they love Me? Do they love My Son? All shall be accountable for what they have been given. I will request My return from what I have entrusted them with. Faithful is he who has willingly submitted to Me, My Spirit and to My Word. My Word, not man's! My truth, not the impostors'! My Spirit, not the false ones'! For I shall take account of all debts not forgiven or released. In My hand are the scales of justice and righteousness. None shall be taken from Me which is Mine." He closes His hand and sits back.

"My Word remains. My Son has fulfilled and proclaimed My truth as I have given it to Him. It shall stand."

Dialogue 33

Victory Over Lies

"For a day in your courts is better than a thousand. I would rather be a doorkeeper in the house of my God, than to dwell in the tents of wickedness. For Yahweh God is a sun and a shield. Yahweh will give grace and glory. He withholds no good thing from those who walk blamelessly. Yahweh of Armies, blessed is the man who trusts in you." - Psalm 84:10-12 (WEB)

The Anticipation

"Yahweh of Armies, blessed is the man who trusts in you." - Psalm 84:12 (WEB)

The Biblical word for obey comes from the Greek word "hupakou" which means to listen attentively. It means to actively follow a command, and in order to do that you have to pay attention. Why do you think some people choose to obey and others do not? How can trust be a factor in a person's choice to obey or not?

The Apostle James declared in James 2:18 that he would show you his faith by his works. What do you think that means? Look at James 2:14-22, how can obedience be a form of faith?

Blessed is the man who not only believes God, but also trusts in Him with an obedient heart. John 14:18-26 declares that God will not leave us as orphans, but that he will send us a helper to teach us and help us to do His Word. Who else does God provide to help us? (Ephesians 4:11-16)

The Conversation

"Remember, faithfulness is the obedience from the love that overflows from within."

Lord, You also have said worship is the overflow of love from within.

"Yes, and so is obedience and faithfulness. One cannot be faithful as I have designed faith to be, without love. Faith, My child, is more than sitting on a chair you believe is safe as you have learned. Faith stands, even when everything perceived tells you not to. Each stand grows, stretches, and strengthens one's faith."

I see an entrance where a small enemy was let in by the guard. I realize this small enemy represents a little lie. Now, because the small lie was let in, a larger one is let in with the help of the smaller one. Next, a larger one comes in and together they are able to just bulldoze through the guard and everyone else in the way. I understand if the guard had stood against the small, initial lie, he could have stood later and not fallen under the force of the greater ones. Because of his carelessness, his focus was diverted and chaos overtook easily.

"Faith is the same. When it is diverted, it cannot stand. Yes, that is why when one is tossed about as the waves, it is dangerous." (See James 1:2-8)

I see, doubt is faith diverted. Doubt is when we take our focus off God and His truth. This causes one to begin to be tossed to and fro. Once unsteady, the rest of the attack can do more damage because of the growing force and this can cause one to become even more unstable.

"When you doubt My word, even in the slightest way, the enemy can walk in ever so small and insignificant. Then he diverts your attention for the next lie. Soon you are filled with chaos and uncertainty. Even with My Word, you can no longer stand. You are about to be bulldozed. The enemy knows how this works. He then retrains and resets the foundation with his lies and his design."

When the enemy has replaced Your truth with his lies, then all that is built upon the foundation is unstable. It can destroy the person as well as others.

How then, Lord, can one demolish the enemy's encampment within a person? Every lie is so entangled and woven with the other lies. It is hard to identify and isolate them. It is like they hold each other up.

"They stand only by the faith of the one who desires them to be truth."

Is there an element of pride?

"An element of pride starts as an infant, innocent and trusting. Then, as it grows in stature and in knowledge, it establishes itself in authority. This then soon becomes a bulwark within one's life and becomes the standard of his faith."

"To break the stronghold, a man must admit his dependence upon Me for the truth. Discernment is only through My Spirit and My Word. From a man's heart is the beginning of his truth, not his mind. If pride is in the heart, it does not matter what the truth is in his mind. It shall be used through the intent of the heart. When one comes before Me in humility and subjection, only then can he accept correction, rebuke, and reproof. He needs to be willing to surrender any understanding or presupposition regardless of the ties to any other knowledge or concept it may have. When he allows his beliefs to crumble before Me, then he can allow me to rebuild with the truth from Jesus as the foundation. Many have the tendency to pick up the crumbles that remain scattered about to rebuild. When this is done with one's own understanding, the design is flawed which soon creates conflict within. One needs to walk with Me, be patient and allow Me to teach him, with the help of those who are Mine. He needs to continue to be humble and submissive to Me and others. This is why even My teachers and leaders must be humble and teachable, for pride destroys, not only themselves, but others as well."

Lord, I see the truth and wisdom in what you are saying, but there is also a fear that what we might embrace or learn will be false teaching. It is difficult to surrender what is comfortable and known for fear of getting lost. How do we discern false teaching? How do You help us recognize what doesn't come from You and what does? Obviously any teaching needs to match up with Scripture and bring You glory according to I John 4:1-3. We know that You will be true to Your Word and nature.

"Those who desire to walk with Me will have within them a desire to walk with those whom I appoint to walk with them. I place around my children teachers, evangelists, leaders and servers. With diverse needs and gifts, My children can learn not only more of who I am, but also their part in My church/family. They are stretched and taught, encouraged and corrected, loved and forgiven so they can grow closer to Me. When they seek and desire My truth, they shall find Me in the congregation of My faithful ones. I bring them to the body, the enemy lures them away."

As He finished speaking I saw a festered wound appear before me with a foreign object in it.

"How do you heal it?"

As I thought about the wound that had appeared before me with the foreign object in it. I knew that emotional and spiritual wounds can be made worse by lies and false teaching. These untruths are like foreign objects to a believer and they cause us harm, interfere with our healing. The lies would have to be patiently replaced with God's truth. With this in mind I answered Him.

First, remove the object, then apply a healing balm on it, next wrap the wound and allow time for healing to take place. While the wound heals, it is important to keep the wound safe and clean.

"They must first be willing to let you help them. If they won't let you help them, they will run away from you. If you force them, they will be worse than they were before, because the enemy will cause them greater pressure."

I understand. When we teach, encourage and correct we need to make sure the individual is ready to receive the help from us, otherwise they will most likely seek to avoid us and thus become more exposed to the lies of the enemy. Separated from others we are like a soldier caught behind enemy lines, exposed and vulnerable we can become an easy target.

"Remember, I send My people out two by two, unified in My Kingdom to grow and to multiply. Alone, inevitably they will fall."

I see Your wisdom in not sending us out alone.

Dialogue 34

Repentance in the Heart

"Then Jesus said to them, 'All of you will be made to stumble because of me tonight, for it is written, 'I will strike the shepherd, and the sheep of the flock will be scattered.' But after I am raised up, I will go before you into Galilee.'

But Peter answered him, 'Even if all will be made to stumble because of you, I will never be made to stumble.'

Jesus said to him, 'Most certainly I tell you that tonight, before the rooster crows, you will deny me three times.'

Peter said to him, 'Even if I must die with you, I will not deny you.' All of the disciples also said likewise." - Matthew 26:31-35 (WEB)

The Anticipation

"Peter said to him, 'Even if I must die with you, I will not deny you.' All of the disciples also said likewise." - Matthew 26:35 (WEB)

Peter's devotion to Jesus was so great He couldn't imagine ever denying Him. Yet that was exactly what he did just hours later and he wept bitterly because of it. (Read what happened in Matthew 26:69-75.) In what ways do we deny that we follow Jesus?

Look at Matthew 10:32, 33. In light of this Scripture what would you expect to happen to Peter?

In John 21:15-19 we see Jesus restore Peter. Why do you think Jesus restored him?

The Conversation

Lord, You are holy and true, there is none like You. You stand in all Your glory, perfect in righteousness. I praise You for all You are! Your goodness shines beyond the heavens and Your mercies upon the souls of men. You are high and lifted up. And yet, You bid us to come to You. I come to You because I love You and proclaim You as the Most High God!

"My child, you are becoming brighter and brighter every day because you have sought Me in Spirit and in truth. Even those days when you struggle to stay near Me, I am never far away. My promise stands true, I am with you to the ends of the earth. Nothing can separate us. Yes, that is right, as long as you desire Me and My love, nothing can take you away from Me. Your choice, My power. Your will, My strength. For I desire all men to come to Me. Whoever calls upon My name, I will bring to Me. Just like I invited them on the mountain with Moses and Aaron, I invite everyone to My Holy Mountain. Many fear Me and do not trust Me. Not all who were at the base of the mountain rejected Me for the golden calf. There was a remnant who stayed faithful, I know who they are. Those who come unto Me in Spirit and in truth while loving Me with their whole heart, they are My elect. They have seen Me, they have heard Me, they have touched Me. The reason they are safe is because they know what they surrender if they walk away from Me. They know the truth. Anyone who denies Me before man, I will deny before My Father and the hosts before His throne."

What about Peter, Lord? He denied You three times.

"Peter had been established by My authority which he placed himself under. He was convicted immediately and humbled himself before the Living God in his shame. He was as the prodigal son, repentant desiring only to be the smallest in his Father's home. His love for Me never wavered, even though he struggled being Mine for a short time. You see, I know the heart, I know the desires and thoughts within a man even more than man knows his own heart and mind. There is not always a clear line like the base of the mountain. There is much testing and purification that happens between a man and Myself whom others do not see. Thus, all must be careful not to judge a man's heart, for I am the only one who can judge in righteousness and truth. Judge a man's actions and his words, but only in love. One can see truth when he looks through the eyes of love. Is that not how I look upon man, for I am love?"

"Know this, I am God. The God of Abraham, Isaac and Jacob. I will achieve My perfect will regardless of man's works, desires or influence. No man can thwart, push aside or halt My purpose and will. Who is man anyway? I created him and without Me he is nothing but the dust in the wind. He is dead without Me."

Dialogue 35

Eternal Consequences of Our Judgments

"He opened his mouth and taught them, saying, 'Blessed are the poor in spirit, for theirs is the Kingdom of Heaven. Blessed are those who mourn, for they shall be comforted. Blessed are the gentle, for they shall inherit the earth. Blessed are those who hunger and thirst after righteousness, for they shall be filled. Blessed are the merciful, for they shall obtain mercy. Blessed are the pure in heart, for they shall see God. Blessed are the peacemakers, for they shall be called children of God. Blessed are those who have been persecuted for righteousness' sake, for theirs is the Kingdom of Heaven. Blessed are you when people reproach you, persecute you, and say all kinds of evil against you falsely, for my sake.'" - Matthew 5:2-11 (WEB)

The Anticipation

"Blessed are the gentle, for they shall inherit the earth." - Matthew 5:5 (WEB)

Gentleness is sometimes described as being tender, kind, considerate, mild, and sweet tempered. How do you define gentleness? Compare that to the concept of meekness, which is seen as submissive, gentle and quiet in spirit.

Isaiah 11:1-5 gives us characteristics of the Messiah. According to verses 3 and 4, how does the promised Messiah rule or judge? Who will He rule in favor of?

Pride stands in direct opposition to meekness. How does God feel about pride? See Proverbs 16:5

The Conversation

"The just shall live by faith. I shall sing over My righteous ones with songs of rejoicing. The greatness of what I speak is rarely seen in its fullness from the perspective of man, for man cannot fathom the depths of understanding I possess. Nor do most want to for they take what I have spoken and make it fit their own agenda. It has been modeled before man and child how to read My word for their own use and understanding. For that I am angry. My people lack not only the depth of My truth, but also the basic truths that Jesus taught. My word is treated as a tool to be used at certain applications, but not for the totality of who they are or their life."

"Child, it is all about the heart. When those who love Me and desire to obey Me slip, I am there to quickly catch them and bring them back to Me, for they desire to be near Me. For others who call Me Lord, yet seek ways to live their lives as their own, I will let them go. At first I will try to bring them back, but if they fight and rebel, then how can I force them to stay at My side? Yes, I am patient with My elect, for they long to be with Me and to obey Me. That is how you will know who the elect are, they shine brightly because of their love for Me and for others. They are humble and serving, they are teachable and quiet in spirit. For My own, I shall preserve in ways beyond expectations as a testimony to who I am."

"There is a difference between ones whose mouths sing to Me and those whose hearts raise up in song. The last will be first and the first will be last."

I see before me a group of Christians standing on a hill looking below them at a variety of people with different denominational beliefs, financial statuses, and cultural diversities. The ones on the hill were judging those below them and casting stones down on the ones they were proclaiming judgment and heresy upon, even though they are brothers. In the eyes of those on the hill, they are better, more righteous, and closer to God.

As I look closer at those who were being attacked in the valley, they continue to be gentle and humble as they continue to serve each other and God. While they worked, they would look up with great love at the ones who are casting stones upon them.

"The meek shall inherit the earth, all I have belongs to them. The ones who love Me and love others, they are My elect. They are Mine! The others shall be judged according to the pronouncement upon their lips and the intent within their hearts. My truth will be their mirror. Child, forgive them so they may see the fruit of repentance and forgiveness. Love them with My love so they may see what light the darkness around them attempts to destroy. Have patience with them, yet stand on My truth to proclaim. This is why each shall be accountable for his words. And, yes, I do forgive and remove as far away as the east is from the west the sins of those who love Me and seek My forgiveness, those who forgive others as I have forgiven them." (Matthew 6:14, 15, Psalm 103:11, 12)

Dialogue 36

Freedom in His Covenant of Love

"Behold, the days come, says Yahweh, that I will make a new covenant with the house of Israel, and with the house of Judah: not according to the covenant that I made with their fathers in the day that I took them by the hand to bring them out of the land of Egypt; which my covenant they broke, although I was a husband to them, says Yahweh. But this is the covenant that I will make with the house of Israel after those days, says Yahweh: I will put my law in their inward parts, and in their heart will I write it; and I will be their God, and they shall be my people." - Jeremiah 31:31-33 (WEB)

The Anticipation

"I will put my law in their inward parts, and in their heart will I write it; and I will be their God, and they shall be my people" - Jeremiah 31:33(b) (WEB)

Even if you do not know much about the Bible at this point, what value do you see in God placing His law in man's heart versus on stone tablets like the 10 commandments?

In what ways have you experienced conviction or the understanding that what you have done or are doing is sin in God's eyes?

What are your normal responses when you are convicted?

The Conversation

"I Am. I am from the Father, given for you. Eat of Me."

As He offers the bread, somehow I know He means more than what I have realized before.

"This is My covenant. I offer it to you. Receive. Enter into My covenant. Drink."

As I receive the cup from His hand, I understand Jesus is revealing a tremendous truth to me. This is His New Covenant. Not like the covenant He made before, not like the one written on stone tablets. This covenant is intended for our hearts, it is something brand new and lasting for He has made the first one old and already it is vanishing. Now, we can obey out of fear for whatever we think we must obey and do; or we can choose to love Jesus with all our heart, soul, and mind while trusting He is enough. Jesus is the mediator of this New Covenant and the blood He shed for our sins is superior to the Old Covenant. He died that we might have life, that we might be one with Him. When we love and trust Jesus, we find freedom and a deeper communion with Him as our Lord, and our friend. In return He teaches and equips us to love others.

Jesus, I want to thank You for Your Scriptures, for Your words and the truths You have shared. You have taught me so much regarding I John chapters 4 and 5 about loving our brother whom we do see otherwise we cannot love You whom we do not see. You have revealed Your love in my life through my family, friends and church. Thank you so much for helping me to grow in love. I have grown deeper in my relationships here on the earth as well as in my relationship with You. You have also taught me the freedom and joy found in pure love. Lord, help me to love my family so as to teach them too of the depth and width and height of Your love for them, as well as the love we can have with each other. You are the Most High God, above all we could ever know. I trust You! I want to love You Lord as You desire to be loved by Your people.

"You are no longer slaves, you are My friends."

You sit at the right hand of God our Father. You are our High Priest and our King. How can we understand Your role and yet have a relationship to You as a friend also? Help me understand so I can teach and proclaim Your desire for a relationship with us. I know what I have been taught by man, You teach me now, please. I want Your truth, not man's understanding.

"Remember Eden? Remember the testimony that I walked with and talked with Adam and Eve. We shared time, conversation, intimacy with each other. We had a relationship of trust until it was broken by a lie and doubt.

My desire of a relationship with them is as it was when I created all the heavens and the earth for man. I wanted them to be happy, fulfilled, to have everything they would need and want, pleasure and peace, joy and laughter. I desired to be beside them as they experienced all I created for them. My heart was filled as they loved each other and Me as we walked in harmony. There is unity as well as a oneness that comes when sharing a sweet joy with someone. When sin entered, not only did it destroy the trust, but guilt and shame entered in between us. These three areas alone can destroy any shred left of a relationship. Guilt and shame build tremendously strong boundaries that will stay longer than any remembrance of what caused them in the first place."

I know the truth of what You are saying from not only my personal experiences but what I have observed in others. Trust is simply key to any healthy relationship while guilt and shame only deepens the divide.

"Strength in any relationship can be the result of control or of mutual humility and respect. Which one would hold more freedom?"

I say the one with mutual respect and humility.

"Yes. Freedom is found in love as I have designed it. Where does My love end?"

Your love has no end. You are love. You fill eternity.

"What cannot enter into My love?" Jesus sits back and looks at me intently.

Anything that is not of You?

"Yes, child and more. What is of Me can be added to, tainted. Look." Jesus hands me a ball of light and places it in my hands. It glows and radiates light upon all that is near it. "This is holy, from Me, My instructions to you. Go, take them to yourself and walk in accordance to what I have given you."

I could see myself in the world again, standing on a street. I knew I had a job to do. I had to deliver His Words of instruction to those around me. It was a message of hope and a message of warning. I see myself speak the message to a group of people in front of me. I tell them of God, of how He had given me the ability to speak and then of the message itself. As I give the message, I can see dark shapes, like wolves, jump out of nowhere to bite at the words as they drift through the air to the people. The words are like small bits of the sphere of light God had given me. The wolves snap at the bits of glowing words but cannot change them or affect their appearance.

Then I see what looks like dark beings wrap around some of the people. As they receive the words of God that are drifting in the air, the dark ones speak closely into their ears adding darkness to the light. In contrast to them another group shines brightly and receives the original words spoken with joy as they are delivered. Yet there are still others who are not even paying attention to the words. The last group reaches up and grabs only parts of what was spoken. The pieces they took then are rearranged, rolled up and put into their jacket pockets as if they are to be used later for their own purposes. I look up and see Jesus standing just off to the side watching me.

"Stay faithful child, regardless of what you see. Stay faithful to what I gave you. Do not respond to what you see in the people, in the world. Only obey Me and do as I lead you."

"That which was given by Me, My truth, cannot be twisted against Me or against My own. I see from above with eyes as a being of perfection. I see all that man does to destroy others as well as themselves. All will stand before Me. Many will fall before Me as they realize how they created their own truth and how it was twisted out of My truth. Trust Me, follow Me regardless of what you see others do."

Yes, Lord. I pray for not only myself, but for all my brothers and sisters who are doing Your work also. May Your people stand strong in Your truth and continue in Your will for their lives. Do not let the enemy steal from them as You explained in the parable of the sower in Matthew 13:1-23.

Dialogue 37

Dangers of Presumption

"Trust in Yahweh with all your heart, and don't lean on your own understanding. In all your ways acknowledge him, and he will make your paths straight. Don't be wise in your own eyes. Fear Yahweh, and depart from evil." - Proverbs 3:5-7 (WEB)

The Anticipation

"Trust in Yahweh with all your heart, and don't lean on your own understanding." - Proverbs 3:5 (WEB)

I don't know about you but I highly value self-reliance. I like being able to get things done on my own. When I see a problem I try to step back, evaluate the information and then form a solution. Then I eagerly dive into the work needed to be done to accomplish my goals. What about you? How do you tackle problems in your life? Do you handle big problems different from little ones? If yes, in what way?

"Trust in the Lord with all your heart," the Scripture says, yet trust can be difficult in any relationship, especially with an unseen God. In what areas do you trust God. In what areas of your life do you struggle? What makes these areas different?

What do you need to do to increase your trust level with God? Examine v.6 for the answer.

The Conversation

Jesus asks me to come with Him. We start walking through a long tunnel. It is dark all around except for the spot of light ahead. Jesus' glory shines around us for only a short distance and I feel His presence beside me.

"How do you know what step to take? In what direction?"

I see the light ahead, so I am walking toward it. I know You are beside me keeping me safe.

"What if I veered away in another direction? Would you question Me or the light ahead?"

To be honest, I have to admit that I my first thought is to question Him. I wonder why He is veering away from the light that is at the end of the tunnel.

"What makes you think or presume that the light is our destination?"

We stop. I look at the light. Well, from previous experiences, when walking down a tunnel one focuses on the light. It is the way out.

Jesus spreads His glorious light further out from Himself so I can see quite far in all directions. I gasp. The tunnel is filled with garbage and debris all around us including dangerous spikes and poles pointing into the path. Next, His light reveals traps to me. Some of the traps are well hidden, some are in plain view. Either way, without His light it is so dark that I would not have seen the traps and spears.

"That is why you stumble, hurt yourself or hurt others. Trust in Me with all your might. Do not lean on your own understanding. In all your ways, acknowledge Me. When you don't, you are presuming a way, an idea, a plan that may not be Mine. Even if I do show you a way, plan or direction, you cannot go and run on ahead. You must walk beside Me. Walk when I walk, wait when I stop, trust when I appear not to do or go as you anticipated. I see all realms, all truths as well as everything the world and the enemy set before you. I also see the people around you, those who can ensnare you and those who can bless you or be blessed by you. All circumstances are viewable by Me. Trust Me. Learn to wait. Obedience is not always in the doing, but in the waiting too. Obedience is also in the resting and abiding. Time is needed to just reconnect with Me, to clean the world off and abide with Me so you can see and hear Me more clearly."

"To know or understand either Me or My Word, one must submit to Me and My ways. My ways are not man's ways, they are Mine. If I tell one to sit and wait while I tell another to get up and do, that is for My purpose and My plan. Man keeps looking to himself and each other for their perception of truth, when none has the truth to give. I am the only source of truth. Do not look ahead, do not look behind to your past and experiences, do not look to the world and man's interpretation. My Scripture interpreted with My Spirit by My guidance will teach you the truth of Me. You will know you have Me because love will flow freely from you as well as every fruit of My Spirit. Remember the definition of love in I Corinthians 13? The moment malice, jealousies, bitterness, resentment, covetousness, lust or pride comes into your heart, you are stepping from My side. Soon, you will be stepping off the path I have established for you. Repent and come back."

Lord, I have always been taught to seek out mentorship and accountability with others to make sure I do not get led astray.

"Yes, but with whom? How will you know? Man has a tendency to find like-minded people regardless if they are of My truth or not. They want their truth to be confirmed. With so many teachings prevalent and easily accessible, anyone can find anything they want to confirm what they desire to believe. Relevant truth is everywhere! One must be able to recognize Me and My Spirit first, then be able to test for it, then test for Me in others before receiving influence from them. My Spirit teaches all things. Know this, there are many false spirits desiring to teach and influence man."

"I will never leave you nor forsake you, My child. I will always be near you. Fight to stay with Me. Fight to come back to Me. Although I am near, you may feel far away because of sin, wandering or lack of trust and faith. Seek Me child, I will be found by you. And stay in My Word which gives instruction for righteousness and endures forever." (See Romans 10:27)

Dialogue 38

Tough Decisions Come

"I have taught you in the way of wisdom. I have led you in straight paths. When you go, your steps will not be hampered. When you run, you will not stumble. Take firm hold of instruction. Don't let her go. Keep her, for she is your life. Don't enter into the path of the wicked. Don't walk in the way of evil men. Avoid it, and don't pass by it. Turn from it, and pass on... But the path of the righteous is like the dawning light, that shines more and more until the perfect day... Make the path of your feet level. Let all of your ways be established... Don't turn to the right hand nor to the left. Remove your foot from evil." - Proverbs 4:11-15, 18, 26, 27 (WEB)

The Anticipation

"Make the path of your feet level. Let all of your ways be established." - Proverbs 4:26 (WEB)

Have you given much thought lately to where you are going? According to the verses above, what has the Father taught and where does He want to lead us?

In these verses we see the Father declares how He has been leading and teaching. Then we see the focus shift from the Father to the son, from the teacher to the student. When you do this the Father declares something good will happen. What are the promised rewards for obedience?

"My sheep hear My voice, and I know them, and they follow Me," declares John 10:27. If we hold to His instruction we will receive life and we are told to stay on the path in verses 26, & 27. To what is the path of righteousness compared and why does it get brighter? What path are you on?

The Conversation

"Trust Me. Obey Me. Follow Me." He pauses, "Chin up, look Me in the eye. I am your friend, I am your Savior, no one loves you more."

I look past Jesus' shoulder to see the Father at a distance. How can we be blessed with such a magnificent God? He truly is the King, we are His people, His children, heirs to His purchase of salvation. What else can He give us? What else could we need? Everything is available to us, we only have to open our hands and receive His offer of love that is beyond our comprehension.

Oh, Jesus, I do not deserve even a glimpse of You, much less Your guidance and love! Yet, I say thank You! Thank You for choosing me and others who are also proclaiming Your truth. May I be found faithful in what You have given me. Help me, increase my faith. I want to do Your will, yet I cannot seem to understand the present, much less the next step. I pray for my brothers and sisters with me, provide for us, Your people, and lead us. We need You.

"The sons of man seem to all too easily forget the source of who they are. All is traced back to Us. We are the beginning and the end. We alone hold knowledge and wisdom too wonderful for man to even comprehend! We are in control regardless of what the world looks like or says. Listen to the voice of truth. Ours is subtler, gentler, more patient."

"Each one who chooses to love and trust Me, We rejoice over. Did you realize We choose to love, and rejoice over you?" (See Zephaniah 3:17)

He moves something like a curtain aside with His hand. I can see crowds of people on a wide road. They are conversing with each other. Some are joyful. Some are in small pockets of groups shaking fists and shouting at other groups. They are all going in the same direction, away from God.

"Many choose to either attack Me or deny Me. There are so few who choose to walk through the crowd to Me, to leave the road and climb My Holy Mountain to Me. We reveal Ourselves to them, but they want their own way, their own path to destruction. They think it is better, more convenient, more fun, more eternal with choices that seem to give them more of what they desire longer, or even just more power. What they do not realize is they that are trading their very souls for a moment's pleasure or promise of pleasure. Many say, 'I deserve this.' Yet what they are doing is trading the truth for a lie. The lie will grow slowly, but surely, to take them from the true path. The only truth is from Me. Through Me they will find eternal life as well as stronger relationships based on the love that flows between Father and Me and Our people through Our Spirit. They will also find impossibilities accomplished, and understanding perfected. That is if they choose Us over any lie or substance in this world."

Lord, I thank You for a wonderful day and all the numerous blessings You pour into my life. Help me to trust You more in telling me what I need to know for the future. I want to remember all things happen according to Your timing. I do struggle internally with wondering if we are not doing something we should or doing something we shouldn't. I come to You now, waiting. Waiting for Your truth and Your leading.

Jesus walks in front of me, in His glory and light purer than fresh sparkling snow. He takes my hand and leads me towards a rocky path gently going uphill. It is narrow and dark. To me it is completely unknown.

"This path is one of uncertainty. It has been laid with stone so you know it is a prepared path and well used. Many have gone before you on it." Then He turned and looked at me. "Many have chosen not to continue or even start on it. It is a difficult road. It has many turns in it where you cannot see around the bend." He shows me a bench to the side, "Come, sit." We go and sit on the bench which faces the entrance of the path.

Tell me more, Lord.

The gold path we have been walking on continues past the narrow cobblestone path leading into the woods before us. As usual, the paths are only visible for a few feet with His light.

The view changes as we are raised to see what the stone path looks like from above. The wilderness is thick with patches of grassy spots peeking through. Glimpses of water are woven throughout the large forest. Generally the way would be dark, absent of much light from above. My sight is brought back to the view of the path from the bench.

"My Child, this path is one of a closer walk with Me. It is not attractive or desirable. It is a path of loneliness, sacrifice, separation from the world, and yes pain."

I remember the verse speaking of Jesus, '*He had no form or majesty that we should look at Him, and no beauty that we should desire Him.*' (Isaiah 53:2)

"That which is seen by the world as desirable is often times detestable to Me. And those things which are rejected by man, many times are of My glory. What do you discern of this path?"

Lord, You know all things. I am learning that my understanding and thinking are nothing in comparison to You. You showed me at the beginning of our journey the dangers of the wilderness and walking off the path. I also have learned that nowhere else but beside You is the path of righteousness. I desire Your path for me. I know that You have created me and designed me and equipped me for Your purpose. You lead me in Your path that You have for me.

"Child, I also give you free will." He smiles. "There are points along one's life to make a choice for Me, against Me or just to stay where one is. Some want more of a position, job, power or money, thus they choose to continue on their own way. I will allow it, although many times I will continue to teach them so they may grow in understanding of My ways to make choices for My glory, not theirs."

"This path," He looks up to the entrance and I follow His gaze. I could see the path was dark. "This path, My child, I offer to you. I cannot tell you much except that by choosing this path, you will grow deeper in Me than you thought possible. The trials will be deep, the rewards great, My presence even greater. I will hold you even closer, speak louder and guide you with more clarity."

I sit back. I know what my Lord is asking. It is going to have a large impact upon my family regardless of which path I choose. More of You, I have been asking for more. A closer walk with Jesus; that's my heart's cry.

Lord, I choose the path You desire for me. The one that will bring You glory, speak Your truth to Your people and keep me close to You.

Dialogue 39

Life's Decisions

"But the eleven disciples went into Galilee, to the mountain where Jesus had sent them. When they saw him, they bowed down to him, but some doubted. Jesus came to them and spoke to them, saying, 'All authority has been given to me in heaven and on earth. Go, and make disciples of all nations, baptizing them in the name of the Father and of the Son and of the Holy Spirit, teaching them to observe all things that I commanded you. Behold, I am with you always, even to the end of the age.' Amen." - Matthew 28:16-20 *(WEB)*

The Anticipation

"Jesus came to them and spoke to them, saying, 'All authority has been given to me in heaven and on earth.'" - Matthew 28:18 *(WEB)*

Do you think people realize that all authority has been given to Jesus? Stop a minute and contemplate that. First ask yourself, what does authority mean?

Authority in a nutshell is the power to command, to enforce rules, to judge over. In some translations the word authority is translated as power. The word power alludes to strength or muscle. It is an ability to control, to accomplish something, to do something. What did Jesus teach Paul about the relationship between His strength and our weaknesses? (See II Corinthians 12:9,10 for the answer.)

I Corinthians 2:5 says, that your faith wouldn't stand in the _____ of men, but in the power of _____. In what do you put your faith?

The Conversation

I sit on the bench with Jesus in the meadow. I am just being with Him and letting His joy, peace, and love flow over and around me. Oh, how I have missed Him.

"What do you see?"

I see brightness, almost white everywhere I look. Before us the ground gives way and drops down as if on a hill.

"What happens when I do this?"

He raises His hand. A wave like a shock wave flows from His hand and into the area before us. All of what was before us has the ripple flow through it. Next, I see flowers of many colors start to spring up on the ridge before us. I see yellow, blue, red, white as well as colors I cannot describe. Lord, I see the work of Your hand brings beauty, life, color and hope. Only You can create something out of nothing.

"What is the way of the world, child?"

The world's ways seem to be to use, to destroy, and to take.

"How does one perceive what is around?"

Well, we see with our eyes, our experiences and our desires in order to interpret the world around us and the choices we must make.

"Yes, but what of My hand? My plans? My desires? Do you forget that I have all authority and power? Do you forget how I fed My people in the wilderness after bringing them from Egypt, cast each star in its place, or called down the heavens to proclaim My greatness? Do not forget who I am and what I can and will do."

"Child, when you make a decision based out of fear, you can almost be certain it will be the wrong choice. When you do, you tend to only look through your human eyes at the world around you. Make your decisions based on faith, faith in what I have said, faith in My work accomplished and faith in My promises."

So many decisions, Lord, seem to be outside the definitions of faith. Where to move? Where to go to school? What job to apply for? How to do this or that? What purchase to make? How do we make these decisions?

"You see the path ahead of us?"

We are sitting on the bench still. As I turn to look before us, I see a path leading ahead with branches on either side. Yes, Lord.

He takes me to an aerial view of the path. It is like a maze. Yes, that sure is what it feels like from our perspective, Lord. Like a maze.

"Man has the view from within the maze. Mine is more like the view from above. I desire to lead and to guide through My Word and My Spirit. Look to Me for what you need."

Dialogue 40

Reflecting Jesus

"Yahweh is my shepherd: I shall lack nothing. He makes me lie down in green pastures. He leads me beside still waters. He restores my soul. He guides me in the paths of righteousness for his name's sake. Even though I walk through the valley of the shadow of death, I will fear no evil, for you are with me. Your rod and your staff, they comfort me. You prepare a table before me in the presence of my enemies. You anoint my head with oil. My cup runs over. Surely goodness and loving kindness shall follow me all the days of my life, and I will dwell in Yahweh's house forever. - Psalm 23:1-6 (WEB)

The Anticipation

"He restores my soul. He guides me in the paths of righteousness for his name's sake." - Psalm 23:3 (WEB)

What do you want? Verse 1 says that if the Lord is your Shepherd you shall not want. Look at Matthew 6:32-34. What are we told to put first? And what is the result when we do?

When Psalm 23 says He leads you and me in the paths of righteousness, a simple way to understand righteousness is this; righteousness is to be made right with God. The Shepherd leads us down a path that makes us right with God and this brings Him honor. According to these verses, what happens when are on this path with Jesus?

Verse 6 says that we can dwell in the house of the Lord forever. Who qualifies for such a blessing? Examine these passages for the answer: John 3:16; 6:40; 20:31, and Proverbs 8:17.

The Conversation

"Child, all the world around you is vying for your attention. What is most important?"

I reflect on all the things, relationships, desires, hopes and dreams around me, both mine and others. I think how I have been struggling lately with a desire to do a specific craft project. Conflict arises within me between how much I miss doing the hobby with the amount of time needed for the project as well as all the other daily demands of my life.

Lord, what is most important in all my life is You. I know I struggle finding You, seeking You and hearing You when I am not in a heart of prayer or worship with You. What is most important to me is to be able to abide with You every minute of every day. Then I will be able to obey You, follow You, love You and serve You with my whole heart, soul and mind. I want to walk humbly with You, my Lord!.

"You have answered well, My child. Much of the world surrounds you and desires to pull your heart and your attention from Me. Many justify their actions in different ways. I will bring truth into one's life in the areas that are surrendered to Me. I can work within a soft pliable heart more than seems possible to anyone watching can understand. Thus, judging is detrimental to the life of a Christian. So are jealousies, fantasies, rebellions, and denials of the truth. The simplicity of a life humbled before Me, surrendered to My will and call has far greater potential and power than any other person in one's own strength. For that one person stands firmly upon My truth and within My gates. I lead and guide him in paths of righteousness all the way to My eternal home. Those who love Me, seek Me and find Me. I will abide with them. Any other trust or hope in anyone or anything else besides Me is lost in sinking sand. When the cry of one's heart desires Me in My truth, not its own, I shall draw him into My presence. I shall love and tend to that person. I shall also reveal and teach My truth."

Jesus takes me by the hand to an ocean shore. The waves come in and gently roll upon the sand. It is a bright day, slightly breezy and I breathe in deeply the salty air.

"Where to, child?"

I look at Him, then the beach. I think of all the ways we could explore, or the option to just sit with our feet in the warm sand taking in everything around us. Lord, You take me. You show me. You take me where You want me to go. Your way is better.

"You trust Me?"

I trust You.

Jesus waves His hand in front of us. There before us are colors and light that I have never seen before. It has the appearance of a galaxy before us. The sand is still under our feet, but where the ocean should be is a multi-dimensional scene, like another realm. Help me Lord, to see, to comprehend what is before me.

He turns to look at me and steps between me and the realm before us. He takes both my hands and leads me toward Him as He walks closer to the realm. His touch fills me with His peace and love that flows through my complete being reminding me of who He is.

"Trust Me. Trust what I show you. Do not force your own imaginations, just let Me show you."

As He steps into the realm, His glory shines everywhere I look. Nothing is hidden from view. Even all that seems to be behind other objects is plainly visible. What appeared like stars earlier are now glimmering with such intensity they are hard to look at.

"The ocean that is before you is the magnitude of people from beginning to end. When My presence is brought into the sea, that which was hidden is now visible for all to look upon. Even the brightness of those who truly love Me outshines all that is around because of My glory abiding within them. There will come a time when each person shall not only stand in accountability for all he has done and spoken, but also for each thought, judgment and desire committed within. All will see every hidden aspect. Is it not written? It shall be accomplished regardless of the lies spoken by man. Nothing can be hidden in the presence of My glory."

I see Jesus go near a bright light. I notice the closer He walks to the light, the brighter it becomes as it reflects His presence. He turns to me, "This is why the world hates those who are Mine. They cannot handle the conviction and truth My Spirit brings when flowing through My children." I recall the verse John 15:20, "*Remember the word that I said to you, 'A servant is not greater than his master.' If they persecuted Me, they will also persecute you.*"

I suddenly feel led to pray for my brothers and sisters. Lord, may we all stay faithful to Your calling in our lives. May we reflect Your love and glory in truth and humility. I am understanding more clearly the command to love, even our enemies, as You have loved us.

Dialogue 41

Workings of Our Own

"According to the grace of God which was given to me, as a wise master builder I laid a foundation, and another builds on it. But let each man be careful how he builds on it. For no one can lay any other foundation than that which has been laid, which is Jesus Christ. But if anyone builds on the foundation with gold, silver, costly stones, wood, hay, or stubble; each man's work will be revealed. For the Day will declare it, because it is revealed in fire; and the fire itself will test what sort of work each man's work is. If any man's work remains which he built on it, he will receive a reward. If any man's work is burned, he will suffer loss, but he himself will be saved, but as through fire. Don't you know that you are a temple of God, and that God's Spirit lives in you?" - I Corinthians 3:10-16 (WEB)

The Anticipation

"Don't you know that you are a temple of God, and that God's Spirit lives in you?" - I Corinthians 3:16 (WEB)

According to these verses who is the Master Builder? We can see from this passage that the plan for the foundation is given by God and all should be accomplished according to His plans. If Paul is the one God has used to lay the foundation, then who is responsible to build on it later? What warning does he give to those who come after him to build?

According to this passage how do we know when our work is done well or not? What are the consequences of a job well done? What happens if you don't do things right?

Look at Proverbs 16:25, 26. Notice what it says about doing things our way, what drives us to do things in our own strength and stop following God. Verse 26 gives you a clue.

The Conversation

I have wandered from my Lord this week as I tried to accomplish tasks in my own strength. I sense Jesus is helping me restore our relationship. As He does, I see the ways I have slipped away. I had let go of my time alone with Him, focused more on things, people, situations, finances, and demands around me to the point where all I saw was with my physical eyes only. I cannot see with my spiritual eyes nor hear God now. It is like being stuck in a dark hidden place where the enemy has me tied down. As I struggle, I am able to release one arm, but the enemy immediately grabs the other. I try to squirm out of the binds, he just attacks another part of me. I am getting worn out from the battle and ready to give up when I begin to understand what is happening. I realize how I am letting a defeated enemy get me down and I firmly resolve to fight even harder to stay with God. Jesus has already defeated this enemy, I just need to understand the battle for each of us is still an ongoing struggle.

The Lord reminds me to thank Him for what He had done. So I begin to thank Jesus. I thank Him for all he has done in my life, my family, and for who He is. I thank Him for His love, His salvation and His mercy. As I continue to giving thanks, I can feel Him come closer to me. Next, I ask Him to forgive me and then place on my spiritual armor (Ephesians 6). Praise begins to fill my soul. In my praise, I sense something is still not right between us.

What is this that is still between us? I see my Lord clearly for the first time in more days than I want to admit. He is bright and beautiful, radiant in His glory. I can feel His love flowing from Him as He comes closer. We sit down on a marble bench.

What is between us? I still feel a part of me withdrawn from You.

"Open your hand, child."

I open my hand. Inside is a dark round item that looks like coal or burnt wood. It feels like emptiness in my hand.

I look up at Him. What is this?

"That is what you have done by your own strength and understanding."

I look at it closely. There is not a part of it which was not burnt. I roll it over in my hand, and can find nothing good. It is very light in weight, rough in texture and pure black through and through.

"When walking in the world, doing what seems best to you at the time, and making decisions on your own, the result is charred bits of emptiness. Remember everything done without Me is wood, stubble and hay. It burns up when tested and tried. It will pass away as the ashes in the wind. Seek My truth and guidance. See what I have for you."

I see in His opened hand a piece of shimmering gold. Its beautiful light radiates from His hand like transparent gold.

What do I do with this chunk of darkness now? I don't want it. You are right, it is worthless. It actually keeps me from You. I see that hanging on to it actually puts a strong wall between us.

"Yes, child. All that is of Me can come back to Me. I created you, I saved you, and am now purifying you to the extent of your surrender. I can do no more. Love cannot demand, only ask or request."

I hand Him the coal and see a dark patch on my left side which resembles it. Lord, take it, take all that is not of You, all that is of my own works, strivings, understandings. Remove that which does not honor You, for You are holy, righteous and all that is truth and good.

He takes the coal from my hand and it disappears from both our presences. It just vanishes which brings me comfort knowing Jesus destroyed it completely. Then He touches my side. I feel a sweet energy travel through my body.

I can feel full communion with Him again. Forgive me Lord for taking things into my own hands, making my own decisions without You and doing work that is Yours. Help me to be able to find You and hear from

You every time I need You, every minute of the day. I need to be able to hear from You so I can know Your will. Keep me, protect me from the enemy and the imaginations of my heart. Your truth, Your truth alone is what I seek.

Dialogue 42

Justification of Perception

"But as it is written, 'Things which an eye didn't see, and an ear didn't hear, which didn't enter into the heart of man, these God has prepared for those who love him.'

But to us, God revealed them through the Spirit. For the Spirit searches all things, yes, the deep things of God. For who among men knows the things of a man, except the spirit of the man, which is in him? Even so, no one knows the things of God, except God's Spirit. But we received, not the spirit of the world, but the Spirit which is from God, that we might know the things that were freely given to us by God. Which things also we speak, not in words which man's wisdom teaches, but which the Holy Spirit teaches, comparing spiritual things with spiritual things. Now the natural man doesn't receive the things of God's Spirit, for they are foolishness to him, and he can't know them, because they are spiritually discerned. But he who is spiritual discerns all things, and he himself is judged by no one. For who has known the mind of the Lord, that he should instruct him?' But we have Christ's mind." - I Corinthians 2:9-16 (WEB)

The Anticipation

"But to us, God revealed them through the Spirit. For the Spirit searches all things, yes, the deep things of God." - I Corinthians 2:10 (WEB)

Perception is reality, but all too often that perception can be wrong. It is important that our perception of things is placed under the authority of the teachings of Jesus and His truth. This passage teaches us that God's Spirit reveals. His Spirit knows, yes, even the deepest truths about God. Yet too often we fail to seek His truth. Examine II Corinthians 10:5. What does it say we need to do?

God speaks to His people in different ways according to His will. We all have diverse gifts and have unique roles within the body, but everyone can read His truths in the Bible. Today, ask yourself if you are prayerfully allowing God's Scripture to flood your mind and heart to such a level that it is forming your understanding of reality. Step back and ask God to reveal the truth about the events happening in your life. Focus on Christ as you wait.

The Conversation

"My child, this world examines itself from hearts filled with pain and deceit through glasses of covetousness. Singing from the mountaintops are voices of great influence. These voices proclaim words that are misguided and base them on selective or partial sources of information. These voices push their own agenda. Balance is found only in Me. The signs of the times are out in plain view; the only issue is that the voices drown out the signs as a thunderstorm does the call of a bird. Listen diligently, open your eyes and peer through the thick veil of noise and commotion, you will recognize My work as well as My words being revealed. Nothing can truly hide the work of My hand. Nothing can erase the revelations of My prophets unfolding before man. My word is true, so is My will. Wisdom is also the ability to look past everything that is either a distraction or a replacement of what I have established."

Jesus looks ahead. I follow His gaze. What was a glorious white now transforms into a scene before me. I find myself standing next to a set of train tracks. The tracks lead ahead to a tunnel. The tunnel is very dark, I do not even see a light coming from the other end. I have no idea of how long it is, or if the way turns inside the tunnel. I stand there contemplating how I can walk the tracks inside. The tunnel is just large enough for the train to fit without any room on either side for a person to press against the wall if a train happened to come through. I calculate how far I can go into the tunnel so that if I heard a train come at me I would still be able to run back in time. As I process several scenarios in my head I realize there is no safe way to walk the tunnel regardless of which way the train comes from. There are so many unknowns I am unable to make a decision.

I turn back to Jesus. What am I to do?

"When a scene comes before you, or an event, or a situation, remember it is not always meant for you to conquer or finish, or to even figure out an answer. Many times, I just want you to wait and see. Watch, be attentive to what is around you. Be aware. Many times people will have an open door before them and they immediately think they are to walk through it. Sometimes, these doors are traps. Other times these doors are a way for blessings to pour into their lives where they are. Still, other times, they just appear because of the way life is. At other times, people paint a door out of a simple happenstance that just seemed to be there. My people need to come to Me, seek Me, ask Me for wisdom which I will not deny them. Discernment of life's overtures with My eyes and My view will grant My children more understanding of the world around them. My discernment is more than they could ever perceive on their own."

"Back to the tunnel you saw. Why did you not look around? You did not see what else I placed around you."

I think back to the vision of the tunnel. I remember focusing on the tunnel and contemplating what the Lord was trying to teach me. He was correct, I had not considered looking around us to see what else was near.

"My realm is completely wrapped around and in your reality. This is why the impossible is possible with Me. In every situation, in every moment I am waiting to love, to help, to reveal, and to give to My children. Yet, they desire to continue with their own understanding and ways. My children forget about Me working outside their box or their allowance of truth."

"So, now, stand there again."

I walk from where I was with Jesus to the scene again. I am standing by the tracks before the tunnel. It is a tunnel through a mountain whose rock goes high above me. To my left is a mountainous landscape rising up and around. Just before the incline rests a small wooden cabin, large enough for about one room. As I turn I see Jesus standing beside me, bright with His glory. I continue to turn around to see cameras and people directly behind me as if the scenery of the mountain and tunnel are only props in a movie. I look closer and yes, that is all it is. I step back and reel from the situation. I turn to the Lord. What is all this? I do not understand.

"One's perception of reality may only be the creation of that person's imagination, or even someone else's. How many times, child, after a situation has occurred, you look back at it wondering what you were thinking in the first place? You wonder how you did not see the truth in the situation. Or, think of when you are told about an issue, but not given all the details. So much is hidden from your understanding either by others or by yourself. I have watched as you willfully chose to ignore a proclaimed or revealed truth as you processed a decision. This is common as people try to determine their own path based on their own desires and understanding. Oh, child, there are many ways man runs through, ignores, destroys, indulges, justifies, scandalizes or walks blindly through situations instead of looking to Me for the truth or for direction."

Jesus, how do we receive direction from You?

He smiles and leads me to a path. He stands beside me. "Stay beside Me, do not turn to the right, or turn to the left, or walk ahead or fall behind. How do you do that?"

I pause and then answer Him, by focusing on You every moment, not letting You out of my sight.

"How can you do that?"

You tell me, Lord.

"One must seek Me diligently in sincerity and in truth. Many times people want My view or perspective for their own gain and not to obey Me. Many do not even realize they do this, but I know the intents of the hearts. The heart is deceptive above all things, who can know it? I do. Remember in Scripture how some pray amiss. (See James 4:3) It is not always that they are praying for the wrong thing, but their hearts are desiring selfish gain or evil results. When someone truly desires My truth with My will through My Spirit, My Father and I will hear their prayer and answer them according to Our richness in glory. That is Our will and desire for Our children."

"Think of how real the tunnel was to you. When you look back, will you admit or dismiss what you perceived?"

Lord, it was as real to me as anything. I can feel the warmth of the sun as I squint with its brightness. Not only can I see the darkness inside the tunnel, but also feel the dampness from within.

"Perception is truth to a person. That is why there are conflicts. Perception is based on what one wants to believe as truth as much as the amount of information they are able to receive. Many will come to you and share partial truths for one reason or another. Before answering or making a decision based on what you have heard, inquire of Me. Ask for My truth and wisdom. Sometimes an immediate response is not required. Tell them you can't answer them and that is OK. When standing before a scene, remember, look all around, and look for Me. You will find Me and you will also find My direction."

Dialogue 43

Nothing Greater

"Shadrach, Meshach, and Abednego answered the king, 'Nebuchadnezzar, we have no need to answer you in this matter. If it happens, our God whom we serve is able to deliver us from the burning fiery furnace; and he will deliver us out of your hand, O king. But if not, let it be known to you, O king, that we will not serve your gods, nor worship the golden image which you have set up.'" - Daniel 3:16-18 (WEB)

The Anticipation

"If it happens, our God whom we serve is able to deliver us from the burning fiery furnace; and he will deliver us out of your hand, O king." - Daniel 3:17 (WEB)

Shadrach, Meshach and Abednego make this proclamation after being threatened with their lives to bow down and worship a statue of King Nebuchadnezzar. They stood strong in their faith in the power and supremacy of God over any god, image or power in this world. What is in your life that seem larger or more powerful than God right now?

God saved Shadrach, Meshach and Abednego while inside the fiery furnace and even walked with them! Are you willing to face, and even walk through the trials and tribulations in your own life with Jesus? Write about one trial you are facing and ask Jesus to walk with you through it. If needed, ask God to increase your faith as the apostles did in Luke 17:5.

The Conversation

I proclaim You as the Most High God, my God, the God of Abraham, Isaac and Jacob. There is none other beside You, none other that can compare to You! Your love fills the universe and is revealed to us through Jesus Christ. Thank You for everything You are, everything You do and everything You will do. Oh, to trust You more! Increase my faith, Father, please, I desire to know and to love You even more! I desire to receive more of You in my life. I want to be transformed more into Your likeness and Your goodness for Your glory! Thank You for Your faithfulness and direction! I am so grateful for You doing all Your perfect work, for I am nothing without You. I proclaim Your Word and truth to change lives, families and marriages since Your Word does not return void.

"Child, you are in My hands. Stay near Me and I will keep you safe. I will protect you. I will take charge over you. You are Mine."

My tongue cannot find the words or my heart the praise that would match the worth of Your glory! Yet, I know that what little I have to offer You is like a gift from a young child and it is precious in Your sight. What do you have for me now? I am listening and humble before You, my Lord and my King.

"Matchless is My Glory. There is none in comparison to Me. Though the enemy seems large and powerful to you, he is nothing to Me."

I see an image of an evil spirit before me. He seems large, ugly, dark and very intimidating. I sense nothing behind him or around him as he covers my whole field of vision. Then my view is changed, like a camera zooming out and up behind me. At this angle I see myself standing very small in front of the enemy. Filling all the space around us is Jesus Christ and Father with their brightness and glory! The enemy who is attempting to block my view is not much bigger than I and he looks very small in comparison to God. The power of the enemy is like a tiny fire cracker compared to the limitless, boundless power of God that fills what seems like eternity!

"My source of power comes from who I am. I am who I say I Am. From within Me all good has its beginning. Those who choose Me and walk according to My ways find everything they need within Me. When thoughts are not aligned with My will according to the leading of My Spirit, people choose for that moment to set aside My perfect supply for them. Then the enemy starts to cloud their view which can become their perspective in a situation. It becomes a downward spiral as they slowly start to understand a situation with clouded vision. Then they make decisions without My truth which leads them deeper into the darkness. They may cry out for Me, but until they surrender their right of ownership to the solution, they are still held captive. All I have, I desire to give to My children according to My wisdom and riches. I offer freely, they must only reach out in faith and receive what I have for them. I do not give everything they think they need at one time. For I know the ways of men and where their hearts are. I will guide, provide, and transcend all their understanding and expectations. My desire is for them to draw closer to Me, to grow with Me so they will not only help build My kingdom, but bring glory to My name. The more one submits and lets Me work in their life, the more that will be entrusted to them."

Please, Lord Jesus, explain 'submit'. Help me understand. I try to submit, but somehow I am not getting it.

"To submit yourself to Me, is in effect, to trust Me. You, see, all I have for you, all My gifts, desires, and plans for you are here, with Me. My plans to provide, to protect, to use, to grow you, to challenge you, to build you, as well as plans for you to love and speak into another's life, are all within Me. I hold out to you, everything you need. You only need to trust Me, to trust that I not only have the instructions or plans for you, but also all that you will need to accomplish any situation."

Immediately I see a picture of supplies, food, equipment, and even leisure items flash before my eyes.

"Not only that, but when you trust Me and come to Me constantly for direction and for sufficiency, when you ask for My help, I will come into the situation and work. One does not have because he does not ask. If you knew that you could ask for anything, for I am limitless in all I can accomplish, what holds you back? Fear? Yes, many times it is fear. Fear of either letting go of something or someone. Sometimes it is fear of asking too much from Me or the wrong thing. Just as an officer makes requests of a higher ranking officer, he may not receive what he thought he needed because the one in authority knows more of the situation. He will receive what he really needs to accomplish his charge."

"Another aspect of fear is being inadequate or failing. Situations seem imposing, impossible or beyond your capabilities or resources. Remember Moses with all the Israelites in his charge. The Egyptians were pressing in from behind. The sea was immovable before them. Spiritual, physical and emotional pressures came upon Moses along with a sense of doubt threatening to overtake him. He chose though, to turn to Me and trust Me. In all the realm of humanity, there was no way out. Even the faith of the Israelites was slim at best. Their cries of fear and impatience and surrender arose to Me also. The faith of the few, the remnant, was enough for Me to do miracles that not even they could have thought of. Sometimes a situation has an appearance that is not the truth. A situation is brought to you; the voices of people describing it are clouded themselves. The issue presented to you at hand is not the actual truth. Many times what is brought before you is a lie to drive or pull you to a certain direction or decision. My people need to come to Me. My children need to reach for Me to receive everything, including the wisdom and the truth to not only accomplish the task before them, but also to positively affect those around them. Every action, every word spoken can be used to draw others to Me and to bring truth into their lives. Words and actions have the power to be blessings or curses in the lives of others. Each person shall stand accountable for their decisions and words."

"Nothing is greater than I am. Think about it, nothing. No situation, no problem, no person, no lie, no being, no idol, no spirit, no relationship, no threat, no power is greater than I am. Also, no collection of any or all of these can even come close to who I am and what I do. I shall accomplish all I set out to do, nothing can thwart My plans. Man has to choose whose side he is on, whose word is truth, and whose promises he will trust. Man was created in Our image, his words have power. Yet, nothing created has more than that which created it. My Word shall stand, nothing shall break it."

"Stand, child, stand on My Word, even when all around you says not to. All around you hear voices, teachings and seductions to step, even just a little, off My perfect and whole truth. Stand and you shall not fall. Stand and others will be able to stand too. My testimony is strong, for it is righteous and true."

"Just as Shadrach, Meshach and Abednego stood, you need to stand. What did they do?"

- They did what was right in Your eyes.
- They obeyed You.
- They knew Your nature.
- They trusted You.
- They proclaimed You.
- They were willing to lay their lives down for You.

"Yes, to submit."

We tend to submit to pressures, to people, to other's perceptions of us and to this world. We need to just submit to You and receive from Your hand all we need for that moment. The next is in Your hand, You will keep providing if we keep reaching out to You and trusting You.

"The gifts I give to each person, I give for My glory. My glory is revealed through the lives of My children. Come and see."

I follow the Lord Jesus. As we walk all I see is brilliant white radiance. There is nothing recognizable to me. I just take in His presence, His beauty and His love. I wonder within, why anyone would ever choose to deny or reject Him. His perfect love covers and heals all that is brought to Him in humility and faith. He looks down at me and smiles. I know He is aware of my every thought. Even so, He still loves me and is patient with me as I learn to trust Him and follow Him even closer.

Thank You, Jesus. How can I ever thank You enough for all You have done and are doing?

"Just love Me. Stay with Me, trust Me. Remember My Faithfulness never fails, for I Am all that is good, holy and right."

We stop. I look around and still see only bright light. To my right the light gives way as a mountain scene opens up before us. We are standing on a ridge of a mountain looking into a deep valley with mountains surrounding us. The mountains are of rock with many trees standing strong and tall.

"From a distance, what do you see?"

I see forests, boulders, cliffs, ridges and how they all form together to be mountains.

"Listen."

He waves His hand in front of us. As He does, it is like He wipes away a layer between the scene and us. I can hear and feel and smell what is lifting up toward Him. The sound of the trees lift in the breeze as a song of glory. The rocks even are singing! They have sounds ranging from what seemed like shimmering glass to the roar of wind in a cave. The aroma is fresh and sweet, it is as pure as the freshest cold water from a mountain spring. All is in unison, all perfectly in harmony, and cadence. I am filled within from the beauty of its declaration of who my God is. The mountains proclaim in unison of His greatness! How can I not receive and then join in proclaiming how mighty our God is and how lovely is His name! Jesus is Lord! He alone has the victory over all that is of death and evil. Who alone is like our God? Who alone has all authority and majesty and power but our God? For a moment I rejoice with creation bowing before Him, declaring of His goodness and of His glory. It is almost overwhelming for me. He raises His hand which silences all I am hearing and experiencing.

"Come here, child."

I go to Him. Only by His mercy and compassion which He has bestowed upon me could I even stand in His presence. How wise and wonderful He is!

"What is it you want from Me?"

I desire to be Yours, called by Your name, to serve and love You. Only You have the words of life, only You can make me into what You designed me to be.

"You are Mine. I chose you. You answered and received Me. You have sought Me and asked for more. I have granted you your heart's desire."

Yes, Lord, You have. You have given me far above anything I knew I desired.

"Did you sing? With nature, did you sing?"

Not with my mouth, but oh, yes, with my heart! How can I put into words what I was experiencing? If I did, only 'Holy, Holy, Holy!' Probably would have come out for there are no words to express what is in my heart.

"You joined with My creation, not in a physical sense, for nothing came from you into the physical world, no sound, no movement, nothing you had done."

No, my Lord.

"How did you join then?"

I joined with my heart. Yet, I cannot put it into words, for I do not fully understand.

"All that has been created by Me, all that has been made by My hand has the potential, the ability to come back to Me. All has been created for Our glory. Man has the choice to return. He has been given the right to choose his course. He can return to the call written upon his heart by Us, his Creator, or to rebel and go his own way."

"You see, if all came from Us, then all that returns to Us would be in unity as My Father and I are in Unity. Our Spirit flows and binds Us to what is Ours. As I allowed the earth to proclaim My glory, it was in harmony, in unity because it is Mine and My Spirit brings it to Me. You chose to join in, because you recognized My Spirit. You have chosen Me. Not only that, but you have chosen to receive all that is from Me. My Spirit is welcomed in you and has drawn you as close to me as you desire. Because of that, you chose to join in as one with My creation to praise Me. How could you not? For I and My Father are One and Our desire is for you to be in unity with Us; I in you, My Father in you and you in Us." (Read John 17)

"Now, look."

155

I look to where He is pointing. The mountains bow down to gently rolling hills. I see thousands upon thousands of people, robed in white, glowing with the light I recognize is from Jesus. They are singing loudly, some arms outstretched, some not. What I notice however is that the light is the same around and between them. There is no beginning or ending or division. My heart soars as their music and their praise lifts to my ears. But, there is more! I smell a sweet fragrance wrap around me, along with a sense of joy and elation within that I cannot contain until my heart too, overflows in praise to the King of Kings! A language I do not know fills my thoughts but I know I am singing praises to God, declaring His glory, singing of His holiness and love. Warmth fills me, starting in my abdomen and flowing to my hands and feet and head. I realize Jesus is no longer near me. He is seated high on His throne, so large and bright, and yet so close. His love flows off of Him to His people as a sweet breath of life. I feel as if my whole being is separate, whole and pure, and at the same time I am connected with everyone else in a way that their praises are singing through me and mine through them. It is like being a drop of water completely lost and absorbed in the ocean. And yet I can feel the entire ocean at the same moment declaring the greatness of our God. It isn't like I am insignificantly lost within the multitude, but whole because the multitude is in unity with God's Spirit! I can see why in the Bible God speaks of many people as being clouds or seas. (Isaiah 17:12, Luke 22:20, Revelation 1:7)

"Who is greater than I?"

No one, Lord! No power, no principality, no spirit, no person. Even if the whole world and evil realms joined forces to stand against You, they would all fall just at the sound of Your voice!

"Yes, child and you are Mine. Nothing formed against you will stand if you will continue to abide in Me. Stay here, beside Me. Stay here, in My promises. Stay here, on My Word. Stay here, covered in My blood that I shed for you, to redeem you to Myself and My Father. Stand, My Child. Let not their voices, the world's or the enemy's remove you from your place, the place where I have put you. Do not doubt what I have done, what I am doing, and what I am about to do."

Dialogue 44

Worthy to Be a Soldier

"All the labor of man is for his mouth, and yet the appetite is not filled. For what advantage has the wise more than the fool? What has the poor man, that knows how to walk before the living? Better is the sight of the eyes than the wandering of the desire. This also is vanity and a chasing after wind." - Ecclesiastes 6:7-9 (WEB)

The Anticipation

"All the labor of man is for his mouth, and yet the appetite is not filled." - Ecclesiastes 6:7 (WEB)

The Book of Ecclesiastes was written by the son of King David, the king of Israel. That man was King Solomon who was known for his wealth and wisdom. Both were gifts from God. Yet Solomon's wealth and position may have been a snare for him as Solomon struggled in his later years with sin. (See I Kings 11:1) Yet Solomon obviously desires to give warning and pass on his wisdom to others. He shows the egotism and foolishness of loading up on worldly wealth and expecting happiness in it. Too often we ignore the words of wisdom in this book and chase after these things because we desire to satisfy our flesh. Name some things that bring you comfort.

"Better is the sight of the eyes than the wandering of desire. This also is vanity and grasping for the wind." What does this Scripture mean to you?

In what ways can our labor for comforts interfere with our spiritual walk with God and His work for us?

The Conversation

"My child, all who seek Me will find Me. (Proverbs 8:17) Those who seek Me with their whole heart, find Me. (Jeremiah 29:13) Focus on Me and do not let anyone or anything pull your attention to the left or to the right. I am sufficient for you. My grace, My sacrifice, My love is enough. The more you bring the conversation to Me, the enemy will reel. Remember the power? It is in My Word, My blood, My resurrection, and in My name. Read the Gospels, teach them and love Me. 'I Am' and I am enough. (Exodus 3:14) The day will come when you will be in the minority, more so than you are now. Your testimony will be attacked because the world will hate My truth. By My words, they shall be condemned for their unbelief. Come back to Me each time, I will sustain you. You must fight for Me and find Me each time your heart hangs in sorrow or fear or angst. Remember, My grace is sufficient for you." (II Corinthians 12:9)

The Lord draws my attention to soldiers carrying men in uniform inside yellow see-through tarps to a boat.

"My people, those who are fighting the good fight for Me, they carry others who should be fighting, but are not. The yellow tarps are the elements of armistice that they have learned to carry them in. My soldiers are unable to fight because they are busy trying to bind up the wounded, who truly are hurting on the sole decision to not fight. As I stand and command to lead into the battlefield against the enemy, My people falter and sit down. They are giving in to not only the demands of the world, but also their own sin. They struggle to see that there is a greater warfare beyond their own self-significance and desires. I sound the trumpet, I call them to revive and fight, yet they only roll over to find comfort for themselves. Yes, I am disgraced by My people called by My name as they lay in self-gratification. These people bring harm to themselves as well as to the rest of My body, like a cancer. I must let them fall away for My body to become strong once again. I will separate My sheep from the goats. (Matthew 25:32) My justice is true, My decision just."

As His words fill my mind I feel the conviction to stand firm and realize how easy it is for us to seek comfort. Truly we deceive ourselves and chase after the wind. I wonder if it is because we think these comforts are what we need and they will somehow satisfy us. Yet standing here next to Jesus, it is clear that nothing is greater than Jesus Christ of Nazareth. He deserves a people whose love is so great that they are willing to serve Him with all their hearts, minds and souls.

"I shall remain the shelter and provider for My own who stay faithful to Me. They shall receive the reward worthy of their calling and duty. (See Genesis 15:1) None shall be left behind. My word is True and it shall stand."

Blessed be the God and Father of our Lord Jesus Christ, the Father of mercies and God of all comfort. (II Corinthians 1:3)

Dialogue 45

Testing for Truth

"I have yet many things to tell you, but you can't bear them now. However when he, the Spirit of truth, has come, he will guide you into all truth, for he will not speak from himself; but whatever he hears, he will speak. He will declare to you things that are coming. He will glorify me, for he will take from what is mine, and will declare it to you. All things whatever the Father has are mine; therefore I said that he takes of mine, and will declare it to you." - John 16:12-15 (WEB)

The Anticipation

"However when he, the Spirit of truth, has come, he will guide you into all truth, for he will not speak from himself; but whatever he hears, he will speak. He will declare to you things that are coming." - John 16:13 (WEB)

Doctrine, which is a set of teachings or beliefs, is created by man and our world is full of it. Some doctrines are true to Scripture and some are not. We should never put our faith in teachers or even institutions. A good rule of thumb when exposed to a new teaching or even when examining an old one is to research the Scripture about the topic and pray for the truth. Do not seek to just support your view, but be willing to challenge it. Read I Timothy 4:1-7. What jumps out at you as you read this passage?

Review the following Scriptures. What common theme runs throughout these passages? John 14:26; John 16:13; I John 2:20, 27; and I Corinthians 2:9-14

The Conversation

I am standing before the Lord's throne which is shining brilliant and pure. Father reaches over and puts his hand before my eyes, darkness wraps around me for a moment. I see the darkness made by His hand.

"Yes, I made the light and the dark in the beginning. I can harden, I can soften, I can light up, I can make dark. (Isaiah 50:3) Jesus is the Light, so are those who follow Him with His Spirit. Worship in Spirit and in truth with tongues of fire. (Acts 2:1-13) Even you recognize those who are Mine by their light. Those who have nothing, even that will be taken away from them. My testimony, My Word, My truth, all that is Mine can strip away the hardness in their hearts if they desire it. Without Me, their hearts wax cold as does their love, for I am love. You are seeing the evidence of it now all around you. I watch as My children desire other than what I have to give them. Many desire a 'truth' that is not Mine. They desire a power, an understanding, a hope, and even a lie that does not come close in comparison to what I have in My hand to give them."

"Hope fades in the lives of those who set Me aside and pick up the lies in the world. Stay your course. Fight against doubt, cling to the what Jesus Christ has done, is doing and will do for you. Those who seek Me will find Me."

How will we know?

"To test if something is My truth bring it to Me."

I see the throne of God as His brilliance radiates like shimmering refracted light. Now I see myself laying papers with words before Him. One paper burns instantly into nothing by just being in His presence. Bright light bursts forth from the other paper and rises in the air to be absorbed into His robe. I realize that all truth belongs to Him. But Lord, how do they test if they cannot experience You as I do?

"They do the same. If they ask, they will receive. Their hearts though, many times will not accept My answer. They willfully, with their own justifications, their own reasoning and their own understanding, darken or deny truth from Me. I have written My word upon the hearts of all men. They know the truth but many do not want it. My Spirit teaches all things for He alone knows My mind and My thoughts. Be careful of man's understanding. Much of what you know is from men and it not only interferes, but blackens or gets in the way of My truth. Also, there is an element of prophecy where I alone know and declare, so when it happens, I alone am glorified. I declare the end from the beginning."

How does one become humble in order to unlearn what men have taught in order to learn Your truth?

"The closer you come to Me, the more of the world I take away from you. Purging brings refinement and clearer communication with Me. Humility and a desire to be before Me in truth of heart are needed. One cannot humble himself before Me while hiding anything from Me. I will reveal it. Most reel from it and walk away from Me when I do. One must be a living sacrifice, holy and pleasing in My sight. It is a process, for love is patient. I am patient as My children learn to walk with Me in humility by the power of My Spirit."

Dialogue 46

Love Carries

"Owe no one anything, except to love one another; for he who loves his neighbor has fulfilled the law. For the commandments, 'You shall not commit adultery,' 'You shall not murder,' 'You shall not steal,' 'You shall not covet,' and whatever other commandments there are, are all summed up in this saying, namely, 'You shall love your neighbor as yourself.' Love doesn't harm a neighbor. Love therefore is the fulfillment of the law." - Romans 13:8-10 (WEB)

The Anticipation

"Owe no one anything, except to love one another; for he who loves his neighbor has fulfilled the law." - Romans 13:8 (WEB)

Lately, the above verse has become very controversial. Many seek to understand the fullness of this passage. Some teach today that we must obey all of the Mosaic Law, others part of it, and some proclaim that we do not have to observe anything because we are no longer under the Law. What do you think? Read the verse again and seek God's truth, what do you observe?

Now observe the following passages, Galatians 5:14 and Matthew 7:12. What do they indicate?

Galatians 6:2 says, *"Carry each other's burdens, and in this way you will fulfill the law of Christ."* How can we do this? Review John 15:10-17. What does Jesus command us to do?

The Conversation

My Lord, oh how I love you and I am so grateful for all You have done. You alone are the Most High God, to whom all glory, honor, and praise is due. You are the one true God whom I desire to love and follow and proclaim. Protect me from the enemy, Lord, for I cannot. I trust You to protect me, teach me, and to keep away my imaginations as well as the lies of the enemy. I desire You alone, Jesus Christ of Nazareth and God Most High! I am Your child clothed in Jesus' righteousness, led by Your Spirit, for Your Glory. Speak as You desire. As I think of Your children, I desire from the depths of my soul for them to be safe and remain in Your hands, even the ones who are challenging and confused, even more so for them. They need you, Lord, only You can help them and give them what they are looking for.

"My child, do you not know the depth of love that flows from My being? I am love. (I John 4:16) There cannot be any other thing, idea, promise, law, teaching, or theology above Me, above love. Love alone will continue through all eternity. This is why unity and love are so important now, it is for you to know and teach. Love is not just a feeling or a thought, it is doing or fulfilling the burdens of the other."

Love is a doing or fulfilling? What do you mean? Does this have any connection to what You did on the cross in fulfilling our burden of the Mosaic Law? Thus, you loved us so much, Jesus came and fulfilled that burden. He rose again according to the power of Your Spirit, so that You could impart to us the righteousness of the law through the same Spirit. And all this is because Jesus now lives. Help me to understand more fully. Correct me if I am wrong.

"The burden of the Mosaic Law was so no man could bear it, and also to realize he could not. To do all and miss in one point demands death for his unrighteousness. Jesus did not break one of the laws and yet, through His love, submitted Himself under the Law to walk through its fulfillment and offer His body as a living sacrifice unto Me. All that He fulfilled is covered now with His blood, sprinkled on each jot and tittle, every table and article of the testimony. Now is given the New Covenant to complete the promise given to Abraham. Through Abraham's seed is the One who is greater than all, He is Emmanuel, God with Us. He has brought the nations into His pasture not by their works or adherence to a set of rules, but by faith in the work Jesus has done. Since He is the only one who not only wrote the Law, but fulfilled it, Jesus is the only one through whom truth can be known.

Deny the Spirit and you deny Jesus' work." (Jeremiah 31:31-34, Matthew 1:23 and 12:31, Romans 10:4, Galatians 3:16, Hebrews 4:15 and James 2:10)

What do you mean when you say, "Love is not just a feeling or a thought, it is doing or fulfilling the burdens of the other?"

"Bearing one's own burden is not selfless. Bearing another's burden of one's own free will is love. It is choosing to take something that is not yours to help another. Remember, love covers a multitude of sin. (See I Peter 4:8) My Son demonstrated this in that He lived a perfect life and chose to willingly suffer for the burden man carries which he can never accomplish on his own. He carried man's burden to the cross, died with it on the cross, then left it in the grave. No greater love than this that a man lays down his life for a friend. (See John 15:13) That is taking the burden of another. That is love."

"Many times a person is too weak, without hope, oppressed by the enemy or needs help to come back to Me. It is more than just helping to carry his burden, it is fighting for him, forgiving him, confronting him, or speaking My truth to him. When you follow Jesus, do what He did, love others sacrificially and obey Me at the same time, you are taking the burden of another. You are doing and fulfilling love in that person's life so that I can work miracles in the situation."

I can't imagine what this world would be like if Your people would live this way. If we fought for our brother and not against him, we could actually be an army in unity following You while fighting the real enemy. Who could stand against us? We would truly be one body, with one head, experiencing victories and miracles in our lives and in the lives of others. (See Ephesians 6:12)

Dialogue 47

Sabbath Rest

"Or have you not read in the law, that on the Sabbath day, the priests in the temple profane the Sabbath, and are guiltless? But I tell you that one greater than the temple is here. But if you had known what this means, 'I desire mercy, and not sacrifice,' you would not have condemned the guiltless. For the Son of Man is Lord of the Sabbath." - Matthew 12:5-8 (WEB)

The Anticipation

"For the Son of Man is Lord of the Sabbath." - Matthew 12:8 (WEB)

The Sabbath is a time of rest. It is one of the Ten Commandments given by God. (See Exodus 20:8-11). Even today many Jews keep the Sabbath by refusing to do work from sunset on Friday to sunset on Saturday. Do you keep the Sabbath? Do you think Christians should? Why or why not?

Did you know that righteousness basically means to be made "right with God". Some people think we need to keep the law in order to "be right with God" and so we need to keep the Sabbath. Examine Galatians 2:20, 21 and 3:21, 22; also Romans 10:8-11, II Corinthians 5:21, and Philippians 3:9. Where do they say our righteousness does and does not come from?

The term Sabbath should not be restricted in its meaning to just a seventh day of rest as many people teach. The fact is that there were Sabbath days that occurred outside of the seventh calendar day. Sabbath simply means to rest or cease from work. The Israelites were not to work on the Sabbath; they were commanded to rest and enjoy God's provision for them. This points us to Christ and symbolizes what He did for us. He was our provision. He did all the work and through Him we can enter His rest. Hebrews 4 tells us to be diligent to enter God's Sabbath rest, which is a place where we can rest from works (the law) and enjoy God's provision for us (Heaven). If you look back on Hebrews 3:19 you will see that people were unable to enter that rest because of their unbelief. Hebrews implies that we enter God's rest only through faith (belief) in Jesus Christ. He is our Sabbath, He is the Lord of it. Do you think the Sabbath could have greater meaning than what is traditionally understood by men?

The Conversation

Father, I am curious, what is Your desire for Your children living now in observing the Sabbath?

"How do you love Me?"

Oh, Lord, love comes from within and overflows for You. A heart of praise fills me and I desire to do Your will, to walk beside You, and to stay with You. Yet, I ask, is there more?

"You could obey My commandments and not love Me. Love is a relationship which is now possible through Jesus Christ and My Spirit. All who come to Me with a heart of repentance in acknowledgment of who Jesus is, and what He has done shall be given Our Spirit. The transaction has been made. What is the Day of the Lord?"

Is that not the Day Jesus comes back as King of Kings to restore His rule completely for all eternity? Is it when all evil is removed so You create the new heavens and the new earth?

"The Day of the Lord is His day. It is the day Jesus gives Me His church as an offering, holy and pure through Himself. It will be the end of all that this world knows and understands. Since there will be no sin, there will be no law. We will be in pure unity, no spot, no blemish, just perfect in holiness and truth. Where does your peace come from?"

Jesus, Him alone.

"Where does your rest come from?"

Psalm 23 says from my Shepherd, Jesus. He makes me to lie down where it is safe and full of provision.

"When are you to rest?"

When You say to. As You design it for me.

"You are no longer My servant. You are My friend, even more than that you are My child. Jesus has prepared a place here for you." Father reaches out His hand and holds Mine. I feel a tremendous peace along with the flow of His Spirit.

"What day do you desire to know My fullness, My nearness in your life?"

Every minute of every day, my God, my Father!

"Then come, every day and know My peace. My rest. My love. Come, know Me. Would you rather rest in the world, or rest from the world?"

When I am with You, I am not in this world. I am removed to Your side which is perfect and holy and safe.

Jesus walks forward. "I am the Lord of all, including the Sabbath. You can come, find your rest in Me whenever you want. Remember, My yoke is easy, My burden light. Rest can be every minute of every day if you choose. For I will carry any burden released into My care. I will also give back anything requested. Most forget that part, I honor their words."

Dialogue 48

Truth of the Law

"But if the service of death, written engraved on stones, came with glory, so that the children of Israel could not look steadfastly on the face of Moses for the glory of his face; which was passing away: won't service of the Spirit be with much more glory? For if the service of condemnation has glory, the service of righteousness exceeds much more in glory. For most certainly that which has been made glorious has not been made glorious in this respect, by reason of the glory that surpasses. For if that which passes away was with glory, much more that which remains is in glory. Having therefore such a hope, we use great boldness of speech, and not as Moses, who put a veil on his face, that the children of Israel wouldn't look steadfastly on the end of that which was passing away. But their minds were hardened, for until this very day at the reading of the old covenant the same veil remains, because in Christ it passes away. But to this day, when Moses is read, a veil lies on their heart. But whenever one turns to the Lord, the veil is taken away." - II Corinthians 3:7-16 (WEB)

The Anticipation

"But whenever one turns to the Lord, the veil is taken away." - II Corinthians 3:16 (WEB)

If you read Exodus 34, you will read how Moses had to put a veil over his face after he received the Law from God. His skin radiated from the glory of God. The second letter of Corinthians written by the Apostle Paul and Timothy to the church in Corinth compared the glory of the Law to the glory of the Spirit. According to the above passage what is passing away?

Hebrews talks about how as the Law is read a veil lies on their hearts. Whose hearts? And why do you think there is a veil? How is the veil removed? What does that mean to you personally?

Why do you think the Law is called the Ministry of Death and Condemnation? According to Hebrews 7:11-14, how is Christ the Ministry of Righteousness with a new law?

The Conversation

Father, will you explain what you wanted to accomplish through the law
You gave to Moses?

"My statutes were written according to the need and understanding of My
people at that time. The Law was the beginning of knowing who I Am and
how to be My people, peculiar and unique, set apart for Me." (Psalm 135:4)

"As the nation grew and split and were scattered, not because they denied
My law, but because they denied Me (See Acts 3:13,14), I proclaimed My
judgment upon them as a nation of harlots. (Read Revelation 17:5) My
people could no longer be called My people, for when they returned to the
land, the land of My promise, they chose another evil, one of worshiping
the Law, that which I created, and they rejected Me. (See John 4:22-26) The
remnant remained true to Me, they never turned away, even when the
wolves and snakes encircled and attacked. They are a witness and a
testimony unto the rest of the nation, even to the rest of the world. The
faith of the least of these has been and is greater than the faith of the great
ones." (See Luke 7:28)

"When My Son rose again and conquered death, hell and the powers of the
evil one, He proclaimed the arrival of My Kingdom with My people (See
Matthew 4:17) which includes those who have been told they are not My
people. The Great I Am is now Emmanuel who will never leave or forsake
His own. (See Hebrews 13:5) They are united with Me and My Son through
Our Spirit. Our truth is sealed (See II Corinthians 2:21, 22) upon them as a
testimony to all realms to whom they belong. For I am Love and Justice
and Mercy and truth. I Am all that is right and good, My glory spans from
eternity to eternity. This is what I have placed in the hearts of My children,
'That I Am and they are Mine.' That truth is the law that no evil can remove
from the hearts of man. Condemnation is for those who trade the truth for
the world and its lie."

"Child, believe in the One who bore your sins and removes them as far as the east is from the west. (See Psalm 103:12) He said you are His, you are Mine too. Do not let go, and warn others to hang on, for My word is true. All of Scripture that man uses to judge others is the standard they set for how I will judge them. (See Matthew 7:2) Yes, I desire mercy and love, (See Hosea 6:6) for those are My truths against which one's standard will be judged. For by it My Son lived and by it My Son died and by it My Son lives again. What other standard or law could there possibly be? Thus, when one loves, he fulfills the Law which is the righteous requirement to be in My presence. The veil has been torn." (See Mark 15:38)

Dialogue 49

Alpha and Omega Never Changes

"Now when Simon saw that the Holy Spirit was given through the laying on of the apostles' hands, he offered them money, saying, 'Give me also this power, that whomever I lay my hands on may receive the Holy Spirit.'

But Peter said to him, 'May your silver perish with you, because you thought you could obtain the gift of God with money! You have neither part nor lot in this matter, for your heart isn't right before God. Repent therefore of this, your wickedness, and ask God if perhaps the thought of your heart may be forgiven you. For I see that you are in the gall of bitterness and in the bondage of iniquity.'

Simon answered, 'Pray for me to the Lord, that none of the things which you have spoken happen to me.'" - Acts 8:18-24 (WEB)

The Anticipation

"Repent therefore of this, your wickedness, and ask God if perhaps the thought of your heart may be forgiven you." - Acts 8:22 (WEB)

Simon Magus obviously was impressed by what he witnessed the Spirit of God do. Yet he desired to magnify himself more than he desired to magnify God for he thought he could purchase such an ability. Peter points out his error and instructs him to seek God for forgiveness. What if Simon would have received the gift of the Holy Spirit to be used for his own gain? What do you think would have been the ramifications?

While some approach God with a heart of greed, others approach God in fear thinking they do not deserve anything. How can this attitude keep us from receiving the blessings of God? Examine Hebrews 4:16, Matthew 11:28, Ephesians 3:11-13, James 4:2. What do these Scriptures say to you about approaching God and receiving? Close by reading Matthew 7:7-11.

The Conversation

Lord Jesus, You have been so faithful to me, I thank You so much for I know I am not always faithful and fall short. Your mercies are more than all the waters of the earth combined, help me. Increase my faith and steadfastness. Help me to moment by moment keep my eyes on You. Do You have anything for me now? I wait on You.

"My child, fear pulls you away from Me, almost immediately. Identify your fear, not only on the surface, but search for the root, the real reason you are afraid. You will need Me to help you identify the root of your fear for I know the truth of your heart. When you can identify it, then you can come to Me and ask Me to help you find the truth to replace the fear. Only I can remove it and replace it with My truth." (II Timothy 1:7)

"Once you have replaced your fear with My truths, then you need to come to Me, to remind you of what I have done for you. You need Me to remind you of who you are to Me so you can avoid falling into the trap of fear again."

"There is a reservoir here with Me that is endless and available to all who seek for My truth. They must come to Me in humility, without doubt. They must not doubt Me, for to doubt Me is to doubt My nature, who I am. I keep My promises to My children. They need to remember, I keep My promises My way, not theirs. Many are misguided or disillusioned to what they need from Me because of their fears or pride. They are short sighted and walk by sight, not by faith. Their hearts desire things of this world and cannot understand that I have much greater in store for them. If only My people called by My name would understand My nature and their position in Me. If only they could receive the goodness and love I have for them. It is like a child who is hungry asking for food, but when presented with a banquet, the child only takes a small biscuit. The child says that is enough. Either the child does not want to impose or bother Me, which cannot be done, or he or she feels unworthy, which is impossible for I am the Creator, or the child is filled with pride refusing a gift from My hand."

"The depth of My love and of My blessings for My own is endless. Oh how I desire to give My children more than they could ever know they needed, but they refuse. They don't ask even though they know I am the one true God, full of all that is good, Creator of all that is seen and unseen, the one who fulfills all His promises."

"The power of doubt in one's life limits not only the person, but what I can do in his life. I wait with a limitless measure of love as the father of the prodigal son waited. I wait for the moment one cries out to Me to reach down and touch him. How I desire to draw My children to My side."

I see before me a dad reach down and pull his young son to himself. The son kicks out and yells demanding to be put down, to be left alone.

"That is why, My child, I cannot just pull someone to Me and express My love because I want to. He would repel from Me even more. One has to choose Me, and then choose what I have for them. My plans and My gifts and My love, everything I have for a person has to be received. In other words, one can deny Me and as well as what comes from My hand."

"Remember the one before the banquet table? One can also come with a heart of greed. One can come and take for his own selfish desires to use his own way. This is dangerous. What if Simon the sorcerer in Acts would have received the gift of the Holy Spirit to be used for his own gain? Many people would be hurt, including him. This does happen, for people take what they have no right to have. They will be accountable for what they have done in My Name, but not of My will. Rebellion has many forms, but all can be summed up as doing that which I have not commanded or not doing that which I have commanded."

Jesus, in the Old Testament, it appears Your commandments are different than the New Testament's? What do you mean by 'Your commandments' in the New Testament?

"This is My commandment, that you love one another and love Me with your whole heart. (See Matthew 22:36-40) My words, spoken while I was teaching on the earth, were the words of My Father. Just as situations in one's life change, so does the course of man's history. The principles have not changed, but the understanding as well as the applications have. My life, death and resurrection brought to completion much of what was spoken of in all of Scriptures before I came. All nations and all peoples are now invited to come to My Father's kingdom through Me. Because of My atonement on the cross, the Holy Spirit is now able to dwell within man, not only for the assurance of My salvation, but also for My witness and testimony. My glory within My people declares of My truth."

What are we to obey? How do we know what you have or have not commanded?

"Ah, look closer. I said to obey My commands. My commands were spoken from the Father through Me as I walked on the earth. Follow them, for I taught of the truth and no one can take My words away. I may change the course of man, but that does not mean I change. Instruction was given for a time, for what was needed. Then I instructed for what was next in the course of man. Why would one need a foundation or a cornerstone if one was not to build? Does one build the walls as one builds the foundation? Is the roof the same as what has already been established? How about the rooms? What about the wiring? Do all the instructions given redefine or change the designer? No, all is needed to be planned and executed with its specifics and regulations."

"The Law was only one aspect of Our plan for man. The whole can be seen when one steps back and looks at the big picture. I am the Alpha and the Omega. (See Revelation 1:8) I Am. Those who know Me, hear My voice. (See John 10:27) My word is what I have spoken and continue to speak to My people. Anything not of Me will be recognized as false for it cannot bear the fullness of My nature, nor will it bear the seal of My Spirit or the testimony of My word."

Dialogue 50

Begin Your Own Dialogue with Jesus, the King of Kings

"For he says, 'At an acceptable time I listened to you, in a day of salvation I helped you.' Behold, now is the acceptable time. Behold, now is the day of salvation." - II Corinthians 6:2 (WEB)

The Anticipation

Begin your own dialogue with Jesus today. Do not wait. Scripture says, "Today is the day of salvation." Wherever you are at in your relationship to Jesus, do not let another moment pass before seeking Him for even more. Each topic I will discuss next easily could fill a book each, and they do. If you need more help or information in any of the following subjects, talk to a pastor or check out a local Christian bookstore for wonderful books. Of course, line everything you read with the full council of Scriptures, not just a verse or two.

Jesus said He is the only way to God the Father. He declares there is no other way to have a relationship with the living God except through Him in John 14:6, 7.

What is Salvation?

Salvation is the gift from God through Jesus Christ so one may be in a right relationship with God in order to enter into His Kingdom. Christians are a part of God's kingdom the moment they believe. His Kingdom never ends, it is for all eternity. God sends His Spirit upon all who believe so they may be comforted, led by His Spirit and commune with Him until they come into His glorious presence in Heaven.

Romans 3:21-25, WEB

- But now apart from the law, (It is not through the Law of Moses)

- a righteousness of God has been revealed, (that we are made right with God)

- being testified by the law and the prophets; (However the Law of Moses and the Old Testament points to and proclaims what make us right with God)

- even the righteousness of God through faith in Jesus Christ (Salvation is only through faith in Jesus)

- to all and on all those who believe. For there is no distinction, (Salvation is offered freely to everyone)

- for all have sinned, and fall short of the glory of God; (Everyone has sinned according to the 10 Commandments. Which ones have you not obeyed? Check by reading Exodus 20:1-17. It only takes one sin to be separated from God - See James 2:10 also.)

- being justified freely by his grace (Grace means unmerited favor. We do not deserve God's gift of salvation.)

- through the redemption that is in Christ Jesus; (Redemption means deliverance from a form of evil through payment.)

- whom God sent to be an atoning sacrifice, (This means God removed the deserved wrath or punishment due through the offering of Himself, and this is a free gift.)

- through faith in his blood, (Jesus' willing sacrifice through the beating and cruel death on a Roman cross is the free gift as a payment given by God. We could not save ourselves, so God did the payment Himself. We accept this gift with an act of faith. Romans 10:9 says, *"that if you will confess with your mouth that Jesus is Lord, and believe in your heart that God raised him from the dead, you will be saved."*)

- for a demonstration of his righteousness (We know God is perfect and holy because of His plan of salvation to bring us back in a right relationship with Him.)

- through the passing over of prior sins, in God's forbearance; (If we confess our sins, He

is faithful and just to forgive us our sins and cleanse us from all unrighteousness - I John 1:9 We need to repent, which means to turn away from our sinful life and turn to follow Jesus by obeying His way - See Matthew 4:17, John 14:15.).

To accept God's gift of salvation through Jesus, go to Him now and just talk to Him in your own words. Regardless of what you have done, be honest and real. He is a gentle and good Father desiring for you to come to Him.

Tell Him you believe in His Son, Jesus. You understand Jesus is God who came in the flesh to this earth, died on the cross for you and was raised back to life in victory over death and Satan.

Tell God you want to be made right with Him through Jesus and you accept His offer of friendship.

Confess and repent of your sins. Tell God what you have done. Ask Him for His forgiveness. Tell Him of your decision to turn away from your sins and from doing bad things. Ask Him to help you to follow Him and to make right decisions.

Ask for His Spirit to fill you to experience His gifts (See Galatians 5:22) and His presence in your life (See I John 4:13).

Rejoice! You are now a child of the Living God! You are now a Christian with an eternal promise! Follow Jesus and He will never leave you nor forsake you! Find a Christian church to learn more about God and His will for you. Read, study, hunger for the Word of God, the Bible. Meet with Jesus daily in prayer and Bible reading to become closer to Him. Remember, relationships take time and energy. He will go as deep into your relationship with Him as you desire. I encourage you to read the following Appendix to learn even more on how to hear from the Lord.

The Conversation

"My salvation is clear in My Word. Come, follow Me and I will give you rest. There will come a time at the end of everyone's life, when each will stand before Me either as Lord or as Judge. If one follows Me and loves Me, I am his or her Lord and will open My gates wide to abide with Me for eternity. Otherwise the person will stand accountable before Me for every word spoken, every deed done and every thought within. Either one is with Me in Heaven for eternity, or one with not with Me and cast into the grips of Hades. There is no other choice, there is no other beside Me, there is no other way. I am the Creator. I am the Finisher."

Appendix

Section I

Walking With Jesus

It is important to stay right with God so you can commune with Him throughout your day. Galatians 5:16-25 is a wonderful summation for keeping in step with God. If we are led by the flesh and its desires, we will not be able to hear God's still small voice or be led by His Spirit for our flesh and His Spirit are in conflict with each other. When we stay in step with the Spirit, God can lead and teach us as well as talk with us. When we live by the flesh we build a barrier between God and us that needs to torn down. God, as a gentleman, will wait and call to you for you to remove the barrier. I John 1:9 tells us He is faithful and just to forgive us our sins if we confess them to Him. Only then can He remove all unrighteousness; everything that makes us not right with God, including guilt and shame.

Steps to Stay in Step with God

1 - Seek God

Read your Bible daily, get plugged into a strong Bible based church, praise and worship Him, as well as allow Him to transform you. Pray often, or in other words, communicate with God about everything. God rewards those who diligently and persistently, seek Him! (Hebrews 11:6)

2 - Be holy, do what is right.

Jesus has the victory over sin and death. Through His Spirit He now lives inside His children. When Jesus died and rose from the grave, the physical temple that was needed in the Old Testament became obsolete. Each believer is now the temple of God. (Matthew 27:51, Acts 17:24, I Corinthians 3:16,17; I Corinthians 6:19, II Corinthians 5:17, II Corinthians 6:16) We are commanded to be holy, but we cannot be holy in our own strength. We need God's Spirit to empower us, strengthen us and convict us so we may be holy. (Galatians 5:16-25, Ephesians 1:4, Ephesians 4:20-32, I Thessalonians 3:11-13, II Timothy 2:21, I Peter 1:14-16). Feeling inadequate or struggling in the fight of living holy? Ask God for help, for more of His Spirit, power, wisdom and truth. God gives His Spirit without limits for those who seek to do His will. (John 3:34, John 4:7-14, James 1:5). When you stumble or fall, remember God's promise, *"If we confess our sins, He is faithful and just to forgive us our sins and cleanse us from all unrighteousness."* (I John 1:9)

3 - Forgive others

Unforgiveness is detrimental in a Christian's life. It is so powerful it will inevitably bring defeat in one's life. Remember, our goal is to be in full, unhindered communion with God which means we must not have any unrighteousness or sin between us and God. Read Matthew 6:14, 15.

For if you forgive others their trespasses, your heavenly Father will also forgive you, but if you do not forgive others their trespasses, neither will your Father forgive your trespasses.

If you do not forgive others, your sins will remain between you and God. God is so serious about us loving and forgiving one another He made sure we understood by discussing it many times in His Word: Matthew 6:12, Matthew 18:21-35, Mark 11:25, Luke 6:37, 38.

Luke 23:34 gives us the perfect example of Jesus forgiving those who had accused Him falsely, mocked, whipped, beaten and crucified Him. There are times where the things done to us are beyond description and very horrible, they will be very difficult to forgive. Forgiveness does not remove what they have done or say that what they did was OK. When you forgive, you are releasing that person into God's hands for His righteous work in that person's life, regardless of what that may be. Many times we cannot forgive on our own, we need God's help. Ask Jesus to send to you the same Spirit that helped Him forgive those who unjustly attacked Him. Tell Him you need His help to forgive.

Forgiveness will do some few powerful things for you. Forgiveness removes guilt and shame for those who have been wronged. It also removes the bondage of pain and fear, releases you from the stronghold of lies and it makes you right with God. When you are made right with God, or made righteous, you can experience His gifts, plans and work in your life. All these are freely given from Jesus, pressed down, shaken and overflowing.

4 - Cast away doubt

Read Matthew 14:22, 33 about Peter trying to walk on stormy waters towards Jesus. Although you may know the story, read it again and think about the storms in your life. When we focus on Jesus intently, the threatening waves that are crashing upon us have no effect upon us physically, spiritually or emotionally. Not only can Jesus work miracles in our lives, but we can hear His voice too. Peter's falling into the water was because he removed his focus from Jesus which allowed doubt to take over. The only successful way of casting aside doubt in your life is by focusing on Jesus: on His Word, His promises, His faithfulness, His perfect nature etc.

James 1:6-8 discusses the damage that doubt brings including prayers not being answered and instability. Satan spoke doubt to Adam and Eve to draw them away from God in Genesis 3:1-5. He knows that doubt is not only powerfully destructive to us but that it is easy bait to use on us. We must always be ready to identify doubt as it starts to creep into our lives and resist it by submitting instead to God's truth (James 4:7).

Section II

Listening to Jesus

God speaks through His Spirit with those who abide in Him (John 14:15-27, Gal 5:25). What is interesting is if we are not led by God's Spirit, we are not His children (Romans 8:14). As we seek to have a right relationship with God and abide in Him, we begin to commune with Him as a friend (John 10:27, Revelation 3:20). Your relationship with the One who created and designed you (Psalm 139) will be unique as well as a journey. As we see in Scripture, God speaks to each of His children differently:

Moses - By voice and a burning bush (Exodus 3ff), and then later face to face as a friend (Exodus 33:11).

Joseph - Given interpretation for dreams (Genesis 40)

Zechariah - By voice, God's presence, visions (Book of Zechariah) and with flashes of imagery (Zechariah 4)

David - Through the Prophet Nathan (II Samuel 7, II Samuel 12, I Chronicles 17) and inspiration of God's Spirit (Psalms)

Balaam - Rebuked by God through the voice of a donkey (Numbers 22:21-30)

Isaiah - Through visions and God speaking to him. Isaiah also saw God and His throne room (Isaiah 6)

Daniel - Given interpretations for others' dreams, revelation through Scriptures (Daniel 9:2), visitation from the angel Gabriel (Daniel 9:20)

Joseph (Mary's husband) - Dreams (Matthew 1:20, 21; Matthew 2:19-23)

Mary - Visitation and discussion with the angel Michael (Luke 1:26-38)

Disciples - Audible voice (Matthew 3:17)

Paul - Led by the Spirit (Acts 16:6), visions (Acts 16:9, Acts 18:9), viewed the third heaven (II Corinthians 12:1-4)

Peter - Interactive vision with the Spirit of God (Acts 10:10-21)

John - Saw Jesus in His Glory (Revelation 1) and was brought into God's throne room (Revelation 1:4ff)

Above is only a small sampling of how God has spoken to His people including a burning bush, visions, flashes of imagery, interpretations, led by the Spirit, audible voice, taken to heavenly realms, Scripture, through angels, even through animal's speech! God can communicate any way He desires according to His wisdom. The possibilities are limitless with God. Do not be discouraged at the pace of your journey or if you are not hearing Him at all. Just like learning any new skill or course, start at the beginning and be patience as you learn to commune with God. The best place to begin is with the Bible and let God reveal Himself to you through His written word. Then, as God leads, follow Him, always using His Scriptures as the foundation and the compass in your walk with Him. Humility is vital, one must always be willing to admit being wrong and have a willingness to be taught. Only Jesus has the full truth. Some things we learn along the way may not be God's ultimate truth. We all must be willing to let go of pride and replace any lies or untruths with God's truth when the times come, and they will.

Testing and Discernment

Test: Warning, not all you hear, are impressed with or think is from God. Satan, as well as your own imagination, can influence your thoughts. We are called to be discerning, wise and not to be tossed to and fro by every wind of teaching or false truths. Always ask God to protect you from the enemy and your own imaginations. Put on the full armor of God (Ephesians 6:10-19).

Use Discernment: I John 4 teaches us how to test the source of all that is presented to us.

Truth will proclaim Jesus came in the flesh from God. (I John 4:1-3)

Truth comes from God, not the world. Everything from God will be in complete unity with Scripture and with God's nature. (I John 4:4-6) As a result truth will always be in unity with Scripture and God's nature.

Truth will proclaim love. (I John 4:7-21) Jesus' commandments to us are to love God and love one another. Anything that causes dissension or division within the body of Christ is not from God.

Truth from God will bring a message of love, order and peace to build up the church. Chaos and fear are not from God. (See also Romans 16:17, I Corinthians 1:10, I Corinthians 12:25, Titus 3:10).

God's truth edifies (Romans 14:19, I Corinthians 14:4 - 5, Ephesians 4:11-14) and sometimes convicts (James 1:4-12) the church.

Truth always brings glory to God.

Truth also covers in love. (I Corinthians 13)

Section III

Remaining in Jesus

Stay daily in the Word of God - It alone is our standard of all truth, know it, love it, memorize it! Everything has to come back to Scripture.

Stay in prayer - Seek God every day through prayer. Talk to God and give Him the opportunity to speak to you. Try to stay in constant prayer throughout the day. (Ephesians 6:18)

Journal - Journaling is a great way to stay focused on God. Journaling can be lengthy writings, but it can also just be short notes you jot down.

Find an accountability partner - Pray for God to give you a mature Christian as an accountability partner who can help you discern and grow in Christ.

Pray for the Spirit - When you desire to be closer to God, ask Him for more of His Spirit. The more you surrender and humble yourself to God, the closer you will become to Him.

Ask for wisdom - God promises to give it without restriction. (James 1:5-8)

Be holy - Jesus taught only the pure in heart see His Kingdom. (Matthew 5:8) Be obedient to the Word of God and avoid sinful behaviors.

Obey the teachings of Jesus - Love God and love others. Our prayers can be hindered because we lack love. (Malachi 2:13-16, John 14:23-24)

Be humble - When hearing from God, the goal is not for self gratification or prideful gain. One must be humble and submissive to what God speaks and to glorify Him. (John 7:18)

Have an eager expectation of His work in your life.
Blessings upon you! May we meet someday, if not here, then in glorious eternity with Jesus our King!

ABOUT THE AUTHOR

Noelle Huether is an ordained minister with the Church of God, Anderson, Indiana who has served as a youth pastor and currently as a music minister. She is also a business owner helping other ministries and small businesses have a greater impact on the internet. Her greatest joy, besides sitting at the feet of Jesus, is her family. Terry, her husband of almost 20 years, and Noelle are enjoying their two teenagers who also serve in ministry.